POLICY AND PRACTICE
IN HEALTH AND SOCIAL CARE
NUMBER THREE

Hidden Carers

D0332299

POLICY AND PRACTICE IN HEALTH AND SOCIAL CARE

1: Jacqueline Atkinson, *Private and Public Protection: Civil Mental Health Legislation* (2006)

2: Charlotte Pearson (ed.), *Direct Payments and Personalisation of Care* (2006)

3: Joyce Cavaye, *Hidden Carers* (2006)

4: Mo McPhail (ed.), *Service User and Carer Involvement: Beyond Good Intentions* (2007)

5: Anne Stafford, *Towards Integration: Services for Children and Young People on the Margins* (2008)

6: Alison Petch, *Health and Social Care: establishing a joint future* (2007)

7: Gillian McIntyre, *Learning Disability and Social Inclusion* (2007)

8: Ailsa Cook, *Dementia and Well Being: possibilities and challenge* (2007)

POLICY AND PRACTICE IN HEALTH AND SOCIAL CARE
SERIES EDITORS
JOYCE CAVAYE and ALISON PETCH

Hidden Carers

by
Joyce Cavaye

Regional Manager,
Faculty of Health and Social Care
The Open University in Scotland

DUNEDIN ACADEMIC PRESS
EDINBURGH

Published by
Dunedin Academic Press Ltd
Hudson House
8 Albany Street
Edinburgh EH1 3QB
Scotland

ISBN 10: 1 903765 66 8
ISBN 13: 978-1903-765-66-1
ISSN 1750-1407

British Library Cataloguing in Publication data
A catalogue record for this book is available from the British Library

Typeset by Makar Publishing Production
Printed and bound in Great Britain by Cromwell Press

Contents

Series Editors Introduction   *vi*

Introduction   *vii*

1   Carers: The Policy Context and International Comparisons   1

2   Support for Carers   15

3   Experiences of Hidden Carers   23

4   Coping with Caregiving   36

5   From carers to clients: pathways to providers   49

6   Carers: partners in the provision of care?   62

References   75

Index   82

Series Editors Introduction

Unpaid caring has provided the focus for a not inconsiderable literature. This has variously sought to detail the range of tasks involved in caring, the numbers involved, the stresses and satisfactions of the role, and the variations in the nature of caring depending on the disability of the person being supported or the relationship between carer and cared for.

This volume is distinct in seeking to explore the experiences of what the author has termed 'hidden' carers, those who choose to remain independent of formal services and therefore very often unknown to the wider support system. It draws on the experiences of 26 such carers, all caring for over 20 hours a week, who were each interviewed on three occasions over a two year period. Their accounts illuminate the discussion of a temporal model of caring which is developed against the backcloth of the distinctive Scottish approach to policy on carers, identifying them as key partners in the provision of care rather than as potential service users.

The experiences at different stages of the caring process are vividly outlined. The author explores the various pathways to becoming a carer, demonstrating that the majority of hidden carers assume the caring role by default. She demonstrates how issues of power and control can very often be a feature of the relationship between the two parties, and explores the perceptions of stress and the use of coping strategies and resources reported by her respondents. The author suggests that for many being a hidden carer is but a stage, albeit often a lengthy stage, in an extended process. She identifies the pathways which individuals may take to accessing service provision and argues that many hidden carers will move on to acceptance of formal support. The policy response needs to acknowledge and to mesh with this temporal model of care.

Dr Joyce Cavaye
Faculty of Health and Social Care,
The Open University in Scotland,
Edinburgh

Professor Alison Petch
Director, Research in Practice for
Adults, *The Dartington Hall Trust,*
Totnes, Devon, U.K

Acknowledgements

To the carers who willingly gave up their time to share their experiences, I offer my sincere admiration and gratitude. I thank them also for the frankness and sincerity with which they responded to my questions. I will remember always how their stories were interspersed with tears and laughter. All names in the book have been changed in order to protect the identity of carers and of all to whom they refer.

Introduction

Carers provide the majority of care for people living in the community. The care they provide is unpaid. They are defined by the 2001 Scottish census as being individuals who look after, or give any help or support to family members, friends, neighbours or others because of long-term physical or mental ill health or disability or problems related to old age (Scotland's Census Results Online [SCROL]). Current estimates put the number of carers in Britain at 5.2 million, of whom approximately 1.2 million are caring for older people (Maher and Green, 2002). In Scotland, estimates from the 2001 census put the numbers of carers at 481,579. Of these, 175,969 (37%) are reported to provide more than 20 hours of care a week, and 24% provide more than 50 hours of care (www.scrol.gov.uk). Many of these carers are unknown to and unsupported by service providers and because of this they remain hidden or invisible (Eley, 2003; Scottish Executive, 2006a).

The purpose of this book is to increase our knowledge and understanding of why, when caregiving is portrayed as being stressful, these hidden carers continue to provide care without support from service providers. The book draws on a qualitative longitudinal study of carers of older people who provided care for 20 hours a week or more, despite having no support from formal services. While not all older people require care, there is little doubt that it is among the older population that the greatest need for care exists. As a group, older people are the main users of health and social care services (Tinker, 1997; McDonald, 2004). The total Scottish population is currently 4.9 million, of which older people comprise one fifth. This means that there are approximately one million older people living in Scotland (www.scrol. gov.uk).

Carers who provide care for 20 hours a week or more are regarded as being at the 'heavy end' of caring (Parker, 1990). This assumes that they are the most involved carers, providing both personal and physical care, resulting in high levels of stress and in most need of support services. Gaining access to these hidden carers was a difficult and demanding process but was eventually achieved with help from a range of voluntary organisations and individuals working with local community groups. In total 41 carers were approached, of whom 26 agreed to participate in the study. Carers were interviewed three times over a period of 28 months. Quantitative data were also gathered during the second stage of the study, with carers being asked to fill in self-completion questionnaires.

A major concern of the study was carers' reasons for having no support, for example, whether it was through choice or lack of knowledge. Was it possible that the experiences of carers who were 'hidden' from service providers differed from those already identified? The study tracked carers' careers and their interactions with service providers and sought to determine what triggers, if any, led to service receipt.

As a result of this study, this book provides a unique insight into the lives of hidden carers of older people. It presents a temporal model of caring that allows us to consider how the complex relationship between carers, the people they care for and service providers changes over time. The book begins by taking a historical look at how carers' issues came to be placed high on the political agenda. It also adopts a comparative perspective by outlining policy development in Scotland, England, Denmark and Germany. These two European countries have been selected because they represent an interesting contrast to policy development in Scotland and with each other.

Chapter 2 explores the literature about support for carers and their use of services. It introduces the concept of a caregiving career and the temporal model of care which lies at the heart of this book. Chapter 3 explores the process of becoming a carer and describes the pathways that lead to individuals taking on responsibility for care. It discusses carers' motivations for caring and their experiences of providing personal and practical care, the defining features of caregiving. It also centres on issues of control and power in the relationship between the carer and cared-for person.

Chapter 4 considers carers' perceptions of stress and their use of coping strategies and resources. It also discusses the role of positive and negative outcomes of caregiving. This is followed by a description of temporal dimensions of caregiving. Chapter 5 documents the process by which carers made the transition from being unsupported hidden carers to being visible and supported by service providers. It begins by exploring carers' reasons for not being in receipt of services and continues by examining the pathways to service provision. Chapter 6 brings together the main ideas developed in the book and examines them in the context of current policy. The temporal model of caring is discussed in greater detail and it is suggested that hidden caring is only one of a number of stages that carers go through and that there are particular times at which carers are more receptive to service interventions. All references to carers in the book are to unpaid informal caregivers.

CHAPTER 1

Carers:
The Policy Context and International Comparisons

Policymakers are primarily concerned with the costs of long-term care (Royal Commission on Long Term Care, 1999, Scottish Executive, 2006a, 2006b). In this context, carers are viewed as an important resource and one which is essential to the success of community care (Scottish Executive, 2001a, 2001b). Thus carers are placed relatively high on the political agenda and in recent years have been given increasing recognition in community care policy. This chapter provides a broad overview of policy development in the UK and Scotland in particular. It makes some comparisons with England and two other EU countries, Denmark and Germany, which have been chosen because their policy in relation to carers contrasts with that in Scotland and with each other. The chapter begins by setting policy for carers in a historical context, looking first at when and how the term 'carer' came into common usage.

Who exactly do we mean when talking about 'carers'? How and when did they become visible to policymakers? After all, providing care for family members is nothing new. So why are carers' issues now high on the political agenda? Questions like these tend to get lost in the busy day-to-day business of policy and practice. But it is important to address these questions when considering policy development in relation to informal carers. Only then can we appreciate how much progress has been made in recognising and supporting carers.

Identifying carers: the historical context

It is perhaps difficult to appreciate that less than forty years ago, the term carer was barely in the English language and particularly difficult for those many people who perceive themselves to be carers. (Bytheway and Johnson, 1998: 281)

Knowing who exactly is being discussed when the term 'carer' is being used can be rather difficult. Indeed, the complexity of caring has led some writers to conclude that a search for a single definition that distinguishes a carer from a non-carer is 'over ambitious and probably futile' (Arber and Ginn, 1990).

The term 'informal carer' was first used in the early 1980s to describe family members or friends who provided unpaid care to others (Pitkeathley, 1989, 1994; Arber and Ginn, 1990). But the term did not merit an entry in a dictionary until the late 1980s and still has no direct translation in other languages such as Italian (Barnes, 2006). In one of the earliest definitions of a carer, Abrams (1978) called them 'domestic caring agents' and suggested that their needs should be explored. Another early definition of carers used in a report from the Equal Opportunities Commission (EOC) noted that the majority 'were women, of course' and described them as 'those adults who are responsible for the care of the sick, handicapped or elderly' (EOC, 1980: 1). The author of the report suggested that the term 'carer' was not entirely satisfactory, but was 'probably the best available'.

Prior to this the term carer was mainly discussed in the 1960s and 1970s in relation to professional nurses and social services staff in *paid* employment (Leininger, 1981; Noddings, 1984). While trained carers were called nurses, untrained staff working in old people's homes in the 1960s were referred to as 'care attendants'. By 1987 the same untrained staff were classified as 'care assistants' and a decade later as 'carers' (Phillips, 1993; Twigg, 2000; Webb, 1996).

The role of informal carers as it is understood today became visible as a result of two intertwined elements. Firstly, pressure groups were seeking to improve the situation of those looking after disabled and older people and secondly, researchers and policymakers were concerned with developing policies and practices. Pressure groups have played a key role in the visibility of carers. A pressure group known as the National Council for the Single Woman and her Dependants was established in 1959. Its aim was to campaign on behalf of the many single and widowed women who were looking after older, disabled or infirm relatives. In 1981, a new organisation called the National Association for Carers was set up to include other types of family members who had caring responsibilities. The following year, the National Council for the Single Woman and Her Dependants had widened its membership to include men and married women, and renamed itself the National Council for Carers and their Elderly Dependants. In 1986, the two organisations merged to form Carers National Association. The new organisation became a powerful pressure group and has been instrumental in bringing about changes in legislation for carers.

During the era when these pressure groups were developing, public policy documents were increasingly making reference to 'carers' and academic literature was claiming that 'caring is news' (Ungerson, 1987). From the early 1980s, influenced by the New Right political ideology, a series of Conservative governments began to dismantle the welfare state, which they regarded not only as inefficient but also as a 'nanny' state that undermined self-sufficiency and self-help. In relation to the policy of community care, the Government's attitude was reflected in the White Paper *Growing Older*, which stated that:

> the primary sources of support and care for elderly people are informal and voluntary. These spring from the personal ties of kinship, friendship and neighbourhood. They are irreplaceable. It is the role of public authorities to sustain and, where necessary, develop — but never to displace — such support and care. Care in the community must increasingly mean care by the community. (DHSS, 1981: 3)

Although the 1981 White Paper *Growing Older* did not use the term 'carer' when talking about informal care, by 1989 the term was increasingly being used in official policy documents. For example, one of the key objectives for the delivery of community care in the White Paper *Caring for People* was 'to ensure that service providers make practical support for carers a high priority' (Department of Health, 1989: 5). In 1995, the Carers (Recognition and Services) Act defined a 'carer' as 'someone providing over twenty hours a week care on a regular basis' and identified three types of informal carers: 'carers', 'young carers', and 'parent carers'. Thus the term 'carer' became a legal category.

Accompanying the development of policy in the 1980s were the feminist critiques of community care (Finch and Groves, 1983; Wilson, 1982; Graham, 1983; Ungerson, 1983, 1987). Feminist academics were particularly concerned with the importance being placed on the policy of community care and the implications of this for informal carers. They claimed that the statement in the White Paper *Growing Older* that 'care in the community must increasingly mean care by the community' (DHSS, 1981: 3) essentially meant care by women (Finch and Groves, 1983). They challenged the assumptions underpinning policy that equated the traditional role of women with unpaid care for children and older people. Feminists claimed that women were being seen as a new reserve army of unpaid labour.

As evidence for their claims feminists pointed to the campaign to extend Invalid Care Allowance (ICA) to married women. ICA was a benefit introduced in 1975 to compensate men and single women for earnings lost through giving up paid employment to take on full-time caring responsibilities. Married women were not eligible for ICA because it was assumed that they would be at home anyway and not in paid employment. This anomaly raised awareness of married women's unpaid and unacknowledged contribution to informal caring, and the lack of employment opportunities open to them. The EOC wrote an authoritative report on the situation and used the tem 'carer' to describe 'those adults who are responsible for the care of the sick, handicapped or elderly' (EOC, 1980: 1). In 1986, ICA was amended to include married women and only then could it be viewed as a payment for care rather than a benefit to replace lost earnings.

Further research into carers' lives and experiences followed and the term 'carer' became firmly established in the vocabulary of professionals and policymakers. Bytheway and Johnson (1998: 249) conclude that the category of carer was initially an operational concept to assess the impact of community care policies but has now become a social identity enshrined in legislation. Naming and identifying carers as a distinct social group has had an important impact in terms of policy and practice (Bytheway and Johnson, 1998) but it has also created difficulties (Barnes, 2006).

Policy in the United Kingdom

In relation to carers, policymakers are primarily concerned with the spiralling costs of long-term care for increasing numbers of older people and those with chronic disabling conditions (Royal Commission on Long Term Care 1999: Scottish Executive, 2006a). The need to support informal carers has been endorsed by successive policy initiatives, which have directed attention and resources to developing support services. The central aim of these initiatives is to ensure the continuance of caregiving in community settings and thus prevent the need for long-term care. In this context carers are viewed as an important resource, and one which is essential to the success of community care (Scottish Executive, 2006a). Thus carers are currently placed relatively high on the political agenda and in recent years have been given increasing recognition in policy.

NHS and Community Care Act 1990

The NHS and Community Care Act 1990 acknowledged the need to support carers. The White Paper *Caring for People* (Department of Health, 1989), which preceded it, had highlighted their importance. One of its key objectives was to ensure that service providers made practical support for carers a high priority. This legislation was the first enactment of community care as a policy and the changes it introduced were intended to 'enable people to live as normal a life as possible in their own homes in the community'. By placing a greater emphasis on providing care for people within the community rather than in institutional settings, the NHS and Community Care Act 1990 essentially brought about a change in the way that welfare services were financed, organised and delivered.

This legislation marked a watershed in the development of health and social care services. It was the first major reform of the NHS since its inception in 1948. Based on the two White Papers *Working for Patients* (1989) and *Caring for People* (1991), this was the first legislation to try to bridge the gap between health boards and local authority social services. Not only did it make radical changes to the way services were organised, with the introduction of the 'quasi-market' and mixed economy of care, but it redefined the boundaries between health and social care. It placed the responsibility for community care with social services, where previously this had been provided by the NHS. In particular, it required them to produce an annual community care plan identifying local needs and priorities. These legislative changes have had considerable repercussions for continuing care. They have resulted in a boundary being created between people with specialist medical or nursing needs who are the responsibility of the NHS, and those who need community or social care for whom responsibility lies with social services departments. The important point is that services provided by the NHS are free at the point of delivery to the end user, whereas those provided by social services are means-tested and only free to those on a low income. This legislation has therefore created charging policies, which have implications for carers' acceptance and use of support services.

Carers (Services and Recognition) Act 1995

Attention to carers' issues increased with the introduction of the 1995 Carers (Services and Recognition) Act, which was the first legislation to accord carers any rights. This Act has been regarded as the first legislation to recognise fully the role of carers (Tinker, 1997; Lloyd, 2000). It gave carers who were providing a 'substantial' amount of care a statutory right to an assessment of their needs, which was to be separate from that of the care recipient. However, the assessment could only be undertaken if the care recipient had been offered and had accepted an assessment of their own needs.

While the 1995 Carers (Services and Recognition) Act was an important achievement for carers' organisations, its value was more symbolic than real (Parker and Clarke, 2002). There is little indication that this legislation made much difference to the level of services provided for older people and their carers. This finding is perhaps not surprising given that no extra resources were committed to local authorities to implement the requirements of the legislation. However, since the election of the present government in 1997, resources have been directed specifically at services for carers.

Impact of devolution

This chapter has so far looked at policy as it relates to the whole of the UK. Despite the organisation of health and social care services in Scotland being rather different to that in the rest of the UK, measures stemming from the legislation were broadly similar. However, since devolution in 1999 legislation and policy for caregivers in Scotland has diverged somewhat from that in England and Wales, with new support initiatives being funded by the Scottish Executive.

Carers Strategy 1999

One of the first measures put in place by the Scottish Executive after devolution was to commit resources to improve service provision for carers. These resources were part of a package of measures announced in the *Strategy for Carers in Scotland* (Scottish Executive, 1999). Together with a similar document published at the same time for England and Wales, *Caring about Carers: A National Strategy for Carers* (DoH, 1999), it reflected the Scottish and Westminster Governments' commitment to a reduced role for the state and an increasing emphasis on family care. In some ways, unpaid family carers exemplified New Labour's emphasis on duty and responsibility as key elements of citizenship (Lloyd, 2000). Thus the Carers Strategy portrayed a picture of formal intervention that supported but did not take over from family care. It was introduced as a 'new substantial policy package' that reflects a 'decisive change from what has gone before'. According to the Government, caring for carers means:

> giving them more control over their lives and over the range, nature and timing of services which they need. It will offer real choices about the extent to which they provide care, remain in employment, receive information and are involved in the life of their community. (Scottish Executive, 1999: 62)

The strategy promoted the principles of choice, consumer control, access to paid work and social inclusion, all the hallmarks of the New Labour approach to welfare. The Government identified three elements to the strategy: information, support, and care for carers. Central to the strategy was a number of assumptions including a carer's right to choose to care, to be adequately prepared to do so, to receive relevant help at an appropriate stage, and to be enabled to care without it adversely affecting their health or inclusion in society.

Another important aspect of the Carers Strategy was its emphasis on the provision of services for carers in their own right. This issue built on the provisions of the 1995 Carers (Services and Recognition) Act, which accorded carers the right to an assessment of their needs if the person they were caring for was being assessed. According to the strategy, therefore, the system had previously limited carers' entitlement to services, and had undervalued their role and needs and their ability to have a proper say in the kind of provision which best suited them (Scottish Executive, 1999: 57).

The Carers Strategy identified key priorities, which included the promotion of new and more flexible services for carers, better and more targeted information for carers at national level, and monitoring the performance of health and social work services in supporting carers. It placed more emphasis on making services as accessible as possible for carers. It was anticipated that these measures would enable more people to continue with or take up caring responsibilities in the future.

Scottish Carers Legislation Working Group

Following the introduction of the Scottish Carers Strategy, a Scottish Carers Legislation Working Group was established by the Scottish Executive in 2000 to develop legislative proposals that would empower statutory agencies to offer carers direct support. Members of this group were mainly representatives from carers organisations. Their work informs current policy and practice for carers which is enshrined in the Community Care and Health (Scotland) Act 2002, discussed below. Many of the recommendations made by the Working Group are currently in the process of being translated into policy and practice.

The Working Group claimed that because practical changes had already occurred as a result of the Carers Strategy, radical changes in legislation were not needed. Their report claimed that what was needed first and foremost was a change in the way that statutory agencies and other bodies viewed and treated carers. Their first recommendation was therefore that carers be viewed as key 'partners in the provision of care' and have equal status with other care providers (Scottish Executive, 2001b). As a provider of care, carers would require resources in the form of support services to carry out their role. The explicit purpose of this support was to enable carers to continue caring and not a service used by the carer. In the report of the Working Group the view was unequivocally expressed that since carers did not need support for their own reasons, then they should not have to pay towards the cost of support services. They argued that carers had a legitimate right to support and that they should not be asked to pay for it.

One area where the Working Group believed the law should be changed was in relation to carers assessments. Under the Carers (Services and Recognition) Act 1995, carers already had a right to an assessment so long as the person they looked after was also having one. The Group believed though that carers should be entitled to an assessment regardless of the circumstances. They recommended that legislation be amended so that carers would be entitled to an assessment irrespective of whether the cared-for person was being assessed. They suggested that the purpose of carers assessments was to establish how the care needs of the cared-for person were to be met, and for agreeing how responsibility for providing care might be shared between the carer and other support agencies.

The Group further recommended that a statutory duty be placed upon local authorities to provide information to carers about their new rights and support options, and to offer assessments to carers. Furthermore, while the Group accepted that local authorities had the key role in supporting carers, in practice the majority of carers came to the notice of health services first. Thus they recommended that a statutory duty be placed upon NHS Scotland to identify carers, offer them information, and refer them to other agencies as appropriate.

Underpinning the recommendations from the Working Group was the belief that carers are in a unique position; carers require specific rights and support only because they are involved in caring for another person, not because of their own needs or condition. The Group was essentially arguing for appropriate treatment for carers, not special treatment. Significantly, the Working Group did not propose any changes to the way in which social care services should be delivered or funded. Perhaps if they had, their report might have been received less favourably than it was.

Community Care and Health (Scotland) Act 2002

Building on the intentions set out in the Carers Strategy, and guided by the Report of the Scottish Carers Legislation Working Group (Scottish Executive, 2001b), the Community Care and Health (Scotland) Act 2002 introduced two important policies which affect the lives of carers. Firstly, it introduced new rights for carers. The Act made provision for the right to an assessment independent of the cared-for person. It placed a duty on local authorities and the NHS to inform carers of their rights. Local authorities are also required to recognise the care being provided by a carer and to take into account the views of a carer in deciding what services to offer to the person they care for. NHS Boards are required to draw up carers information strategies informing carers of their rights under this legislation.

While the legislation itself does not describe carers as 'partners', the accompanying guidance makes explicit the principle that informal carers are to be treated as 'key partners' in providing care, rather than as service users themselves. As a result of this principle, support services provided to carers are now regarded as part of the overall package of care to the person being looked after: carers are not responsible for the costs. An exception to this is when a carer is looking after their partner: in that situation their income may be taken into account during a financial assessment.

The second important policy introduced by this legislation which impacts upon the lives of carers is that of free personal and nursing care for older people. Since carers provide the majority of care for older people in Scotland (Scottish Executive, 2006a) this policy is important in that it has the potential to support carers. The policy came about as a result of the report for the Royal Commission on Long Term Care (1999). The Commission had looked at options for a sustainable system of funding of long-term care for older people in the UK. It considered the provision of care both in people's own homes and in other settings. It recommended that personal and nursing care should be free in all settings and not, as before, to only the relatively poorest older people living at home or those in hospital. Although free nursing care in care homes was introduced into all parts of the UK in 2002, the UK Government refused to accept the recommendation on free personal care. It argued that, given the increasing numbers of older people requiring care, it would be too expensive to implement. The Scottish Parliament also initially refused but eventually succumbed to political pressure to implement the policy of free personal and nursing care for older people. This policy is therefore unique to Scotland.

The definition of personal care contained in the Community Care and Health Act 2002 does not include 'board and lodging' or 'hotel' costs. The definition is mainly based on the one used by the Royal Commission on Long Term Care (1999), except that it takes account of the needs arising from cognitive impairment and behavioural problems as well as physical frailty. It also places importance on counselling and psychological support, particularly for people with dementia. Thus the definition of personal care used in Scotland differs from that used by social services in England and Wales. The definition of personal care is used as a basis for community care assessments. It essentially describes the range of tasks that might be undertaken by home carers employed by the statutory care sector. It also reflects accurately the range of care activities undertaken by carers.

This policy was introduced amid fears that it would ultimately reduce the amount of care being provided by informal carers. A recent study which evaluated the implementation of the policy found that there was no real evidence of care being substituted by formal services following the introduction of free personal care (Bell and Bowes, 2006). Free personal care was found to be very effective in supporting carers to continue providing care for longer, and the researchers found that the volume of care being provided at home had actually increased in recent years. It also allowed them to devote their time to caring tasks rather than personal ones, and in some cases this was what the carer and the person being cared for preferred (Bell and Bowes, 2006). These are important and significant findings given the adverse publicity and concern about the high expenditure this policy incurs. Any policy that supports carers to continue caring for longer, if that is what they wish to do, must surely be a positive step.

The future of unpaid care in Scotland

In a recent public display of continuing support for carers, the Scottish Executive commissioned a wide-ranging research project, 'The Future of Unpaid Care in Scotland'. This work sat alongside the 21st Century Review of Social Work which was being conducted at the same time. Both projects consulted widely with carers and service users organisations. The reports and recommendations of both initiatives were published in the autumn of 2005.

The report on unpaid care (Scottish Executive, 2006a) notes that families and unpaid carers constitute Scotland's largest care force. It acknowledges the need to recognise carers as key individual care providers. It advocates that caring should be a more positive life choice, and that policy needs to strengthen independent living and self-care and improve both the quality of life and the quality of care by moving from crisis intervention to planned preventative support for carers.

The official response from the Scottish Executive (2006b) to this report was published in April 2006. Priority is to be given to four key areas: young carers, respite care, health of carers and training for them. In relation to young carers, the principle underpinning any action is that young carers are to be treated as children and young people first and foremost. Support for them is to be integrated and mainstreamed within current policy and services for children and young people. At the same time, joint inspections of child protection services by the three inspection agencies — the Social Work Inspection Agency, Her Majesty's Inspectorate of Education and the Care Commission — are being rolled out, and a new cross-agency assessment tool for young carer services is under development at the time of writing. The Executive will also consider whether there is a role for a young carers forum and a separate young carers strategy.

The second priority area in the Scottish Executive's response is respite or breaks from caring. The intention is to assess current respite provision, update guidance for respite services, and promote service redesign to shift the focus of provision to preventative, personalised respite care. Breaks for young carers are to be developed separately. The report on unpaid care (Scottish Executive, 2006a) had recommended that carers should have a statutory minimum entitlement to respite. However, amid concerns about the resource implications of this, the Scottish Executive has refused to adopt this recommendation but are prepared to 'reconsider the issue in the future' (Scottish Executive 2006b).

Safeguarding the health of carers is to be another priority. NHS Boards are to develop local carers information strategies, in order to identify carers and inform them of their rights to support, and to ensure that they receive information and advice. They are also to be referred to appropriate sources of support as soon as possible in order to prevent crisis or ill-health. Other measures which came into effect in April 2006 include incentives for GP practices to identify a named person with responsibility for carer identification; set up carer registers; and refer carers to local support. In addition, it is hoped that a toolkit to be issued in late 2006 for community health partnerships to assess their management of long-term conditions will highlight the help which carers require to support patients with long-term care needs. A focus on carers' health is to be included in other health improvement initiatives, in a national Review of Nursing in the Community, and in plans for patients and carers to have access to their own electronic health records.

The fourth priority recognises the value of training in helping carers to develop the knowledge and skills to manage their vital role. Carers Scotland is to be funded to pilot a new carer training programme. While there are examples of excellent training opportunities for carers, these are not widely available. The hope is to expand the availability of this type of training and to develop a national 'expert carer' training framework (Scottish Executive 2006b). The need for 'expert carers' as highlighted in *The Future of Unpaid*

Care in Scotland has also featured in other policy documents such as *Delivering for Health* (Scottish Executive, 2005). The Executive's response to *The Future of Unpaid Care in Scotland* can best be described as cautious. This is mainly because of the significant funding implications that would arise if all the recommendations were to be accepted. Effective action also depends on maximising opportunities which arise from a range of parallel policy developments. Nonetheless, the contribution that carers make to society is recognised, as is the importance of support for them. Meanwhile we can only watch to see if progress is made and wait for the Executive to meet its commitment to revisit these priorities in 2008.

England

Until recently, policy and legislation in Scotland was ahead of that in England and Wales. The latest legislation in England, however, has brought policy in England more in line with that in Scotland. Some of the legislation that impacts upon the lives of carers is integrated with policies for adults and children with disabilities, for example the Carers and Disabled Children Act 2000. Under the terms of this legislation local authorities were empowered to provide services directly to carers even when the person being cared for had refused an assessment or services. It also allowed for payments to be made to young carers aged 16 to 17, to those in the role of parent to disabled children, and to 16–17-year-olds with disabilities. Following a needs assessment, carers can also receive direct payments to cover the costs of services, including education. As a way of enabling more flexible respite schemes, the Act provides for a short-term break voucher which is intended to assist carers with planning and paying for breaks.

The most recent legislation is the Carers (Equal Opportunities) Act 2004, which amends the Carers (Services and Recognition) Act 1995 and the Carers and Disabled Children Act 2000. It applies to all carers including those under 18 as long as they are caring for an adult. The Act places a duty on local authorities to inform carers of their right to an assessment of their needs independently of the cared-for person. It ensures that carers' interests and wishes are taken into account when assessments are being conducted. For example, local authorities must take into account whether the carer works or wishes to work; and whether they are undertaking a course of study or leisure activity, or wish to. The Act also gives powers to local authorities to enlist the help of health, education and housing departments in supporting carers (http://www.carersuk.org/Policyandpractice/CarersEqualOpportunitiesAct)

Despite these legislative changes there remain two important differences between policy in Scotland and that in England and Wales. Like carers in Scotland, those living south of the border have the right to an assessment of their needs. They can also receive services in their own right under the

Carers and Disabled Children Act 2000. However, if carers receive support services in their own right, they are responsible for paying for them. This practice differs to that in Scotland where, as discussed previously, carers receive services as part of the overall package of care to the cared-for person and are therefore not responsible for the costs of services.

The second difference in policy between the two countries relates to the way in which carers are perceived by service providers. In Scotland carers are perceived as key partners in the provision of care. Added to this is the fact that older people in Scotland are entitled to receive free personal care. If the older person is living in the community, they are not due to pay for the personal care element of any services they receive or are assessed as needing.

Provision for carers south of the border reflects the fact that the mixed economy of care is currently more extensive in England than in Scotland. Thus services to support carers are delivered by a wide range of providers from the public, voluntary and private sectors. This is in contrast to Scotland, where the majority of domiciliary services continue to be provided by local authorities (Curtice et al., 2002), although this may change in the future. The latest statistics reveal that the proportion of home care services provided by the voluntary and private sector in Scotland rose from 24% in 2002 to 30% in 2005 (www.scotland.gov.uk/statistics).

International comparisons

Concern for carers and the continuance of informal care is not confined to the UK. In other countries, support for carers is shaped by differences in welfare ideology and assumptions about the role of working-age women. The countries included in this section have contrasting approaches and, in keeping with the UK, have developed a range of supports in response to concerns about demographic changes and the costs of long-term care. In the UK, families provide the majority of care and the system of carer support is distinctive in providing a cash benefit to carers which acknowledges their contribution. In Germany, the specific purpose of Long Term Care Insurance (LTCI), introduced in 1995, is to support and encourage informal caregiving. In contrast, in Denmark, where men and women are assumed to be in full-time employment, high levels of social services are provided and informal caring is not as widespread. Because of this pattern, policy there has only recently focused on supporting carers.

In Denmark, responsibility for health and social care is divided between two separate departments, the Ministry of the Interior and Health and the Ministry of Social Affairs. This situation may change in the near future as major structural change is underway and due to be completed by 2008 (www.eng.social.dk). Denmark takes a universal social-democratic approach to welfare. Services are regarded as the responsibility of the state and local authorities and are provided irrespective of the person's economic status and availability of family support. This means that the system is focused on providing care rather than supporting family carers. Because everyone is entitled to have their care needs met by social services, care by informal and unpaid carers is the exception to the rule. However, for those who want to care for a friend or relative, there are systems of support.

Support for carers varies according to the client group being cared for. For example, carers of adults with a long-term chronic illness or disability are entitled to take up to six months' 'leave' from their employment if they wish to look after someone. Certain criteria apply: the person being cared for must otherwise need to be cared for in an institution, and both parties must agree to the arrangement. During this 'leave', carers are essentially employed by the local authority of the person being cared for and are paid the equivalent of about £1,500 (16,556 dkr) a month (2005 figures). For carers looking after someone who is terminally ill the situation is similar. Provided that the cared-for person and the local authority agree, carers are provided with financial assistance of about £1,000 (11,609 dkr) a month, or they can apply for reimbursement of potential earnings. Parents caring for a child with disabilities are both entitled to reimbursement of their potential earnings and pension contributions for the length of time they provide care. The amount of money paid is based on previous earnings (see www.sfi.dk). Because the Danish system is one based on individual rights, limited use is made of these supports for carers. There is, however, increasing concern about the high costs involved in this model of welfare, so future direction of policy is uncertain (www.eng.social.dk).

Germany provides another interesting case study. As with other EU countries, Germany faced a projected increase in the numbers of older people in need of long-term care services. Concern about the resulting financial costs for individuals and the state led to the new LTCI system being introduced in 1995. Unlike the UK and Denmark, Germany's welfare system is based on a compulsory social insurance system with fixed legal rights and entitlements. The new scheme was set up with the aim of shifting the costs of long-term care away from the sickness insurance scheme and means-tested social assistance. Membership of LTCI is compulsory for those who pay for sickness insurance cover (Geraedts et al., 2000).

Informal carers in Germany have no legal rights or entitlement to benefits or services. Carers' access to any support is entirely dependent on the insurance entitlement of the person receiving care. All support for caregiving is provided through the LTCI scheme. A medical assessment of the level of help a person requires determines eligibility for care insurance. But a person applying for care insurance must have been receiving care for at least six months before an application can be made. Benefits are payable in the form of cash, professional home care services or a combination of both. Cash is only payable if the care recipient can prove that family or friends can provide an adequate level of home care. The value of the cash payment is less than its equivalence in professional care services and is awarded directly to the person needing care (Geraedts et al., 2000)

Only when care insurance has been paid for 12 months can the cared-for person apply for a range of other entitlements which may benefit carers. For example, the care insurance scheme will pay for the costs of replacement home care services for up to four weeks to allow the caregiver respite or a holiday. If cash benefits are paid, then the care recipient is also entitled to a visit from a nurse every three to six months. The purpose of this is to monitor the quality of care provided and to give advice. In addition, carers who provide more than 14 hours of care a week and who are in paid employment for less than 30 hours are entitled to have their pension and accident insurance contributions paid by the LTCI. They are also entitled to free nursing care courses and retraining for employment once caregiving ends (Geraedts et al., 2000).

In Germany as in Britain, the majority of care has always been provided by family carers. The LTCI scheme aims to encourage this, although the focus of support is on the care recipient rather than the carer. The opportunity for carers to benefit from additional elements of LTCI such as respite depends entirely on the discretion and agreement of the person receiving care. The LTCI system does not acknowledge that carers might have needs that are different from and separate to and indeed, might conflict with, those of the cared-for person.

Policy for carers in Denmark, Germany and the UK vary in a number of respects. When comparing the support provided by other countries, it is not always clear whether carers are regarded as needing support in their own right or whether they are seen as a 'resource'. On the one hand, policy in Denmark is 'carer-blind' and provides services irrespective of who within the family might be able and willing to care. The majority of care is provided by the state and very little by informal carers. Germany, on the other hand, expects and promotes caregiving by informal carers, who provide the majority of care, yet policy and legislation accords them very few rights. They are clearly seen as a resource. Their entitlement to support is dependent entirely on the cared-for person's agreement and eligibility for LTCI. In relation to countries within the UK, there are few differences between them, with policy broadly following a similar pattern of support for carers. Informal carers provide the bulk of care, and their rights are enshrined in legislation. They are also in the rather unique position of being entitled to an assessment of their own needs independently of the needs of the person receiving care. Yet, their position within the service system remains ambiguous (Twigg and Atkin, 1994), with only carers in Scotland being regarded as key partners in care.

CHAPTER 2

Support for Carers

The contribution of carers is being increasingly recognised in both government policy and professional practice, which in turn requires greater partnership working between service providers and carers. Current policy has, however, been devised with the needs of carers already known to service providers in mind. Relatively little is known about the needs, views or experiences of hidden carers. If policy is to be designed to meet the needs of all carers it is essential that the views and experiences of carers unknown to service providers are explored.

Successive governments' commitment to supporting carers has resulted in a large body of literature whose titles include the term 'carer'. Informal carers studied in the first waves of research were identified through the users of services (see, for example, Nissel and Bonnerjea, 1982; Charlesworth et al., 1983; Twigg and Atkin, 1993; Warner, 1995). This strategy was regarded at that time as being appropriate in the light of the concern about the adequacy of the support provided by the formal sector. However, the effect of this approach was to define carers as part of the support system of people living in the community who were already receiving health and social care services. This reliance on caregivers known to service providers has meant that policy was related to the apparent needs of such carers. But calls have been made for the needs of different carers to be recognised if appropriate services are to be developed (Atkin, 1992; Eley, 2003; Statham, 2003).

The particular focus of this book about carers is on the lives and experiences of those who do not receive or make use of formal support services. This is a group of people who are hard to identify. Policymakers and voluntary organisations often refer to them as 'hidden' because, as non-users of social care services, they are unsupported by and invisible to statutory providers of health and social care. The terms 'hidden' or 'invisible' carers began to emerge in the literature soon after the results of the first authoritative national survey of the population to address the issues of carers was published. The results of this survey revealed that the numbers of people caring for another person were greater than previous estimates (Green, 1988; Parker, 1990). However, no clear definitions of the terms 'hidden' or invisible' carer have been found. It seems that these terms were initially used by carers organisations to describe carers who did not identify themselves as such (Barker and Mitteness, 1990; Crossroads, 2001). It has also been taken to mean carers who are unknown to service providers and/or carers organisations (Evandrou, 1990; Age Concern, 1995; PRTC, 1998a; Crossroads, 2001; Eley, 2003). Because of this uncertainty about the precise meaning of these terms, the present study uses the term 'hidden carer' to identify individuals who were providing care for another person and who were unsupported by formal service providers.

Service support for carers

The provision of care can be very stressful for caregivers and can contribute to long-term health and financial problems (Evandrou, 1995,1996; Hutton and Hirst, 2001). Policy has therefore recognised the need to support informal carers, and a key objective has been to improve service provision for them. Consequently, formal service interventions have been developed to support their role.

What is meant by support? Support is an inclusive term, which in the present study is taken to mean any service whose purpose is to provide either practical or emotional support for caregiving. Support has also been defined as any intervention which helps carers to take up, to continue or to end the caregiver role (Askham, 1998). Formal services are taken to mean those that may be provided, funded and/or arranged by statutory and voluntary agencies.

Service support for carers remains problematic, despite more than a decade of campaigning, the raised profile of carers and the policy and practice initiatives that have been developed (Parker and Clarke, 2002). These initiatives have been underpinned by an assumption that support services will reduce the negative impact of caregiving, thereby enabling carers to provide quality care for a longer period. This assumption has been supported by research, which has shown that service intervention can prevent the breakdown of care and reduce admissions to long-term care (Twigg et al., 1990; Wright, 2000; Clarke et al., 2003), reduce carers' stress levels and improve the quality of carers' lives (Wright, 1986; Gilleard, 1987, Perring et al., 1990; Clarke, 1994; Levin et al., 1994).

However, the relationship between carers and service providers is unclear and ambiguous (Twigg, 1989, 1992; Twigg and Atkin, 1994). Carers are neither clients nor patients and their position within the service system is simply by virtue of their relationship with the care recipient, who may be regarded as a client. As a consequence, carers have, until recently, rarely been the direct focus of service intervention. Twigg (1989, 1992) has conceptualised these ambiguities in terms of four models of how service providers relate to carers: as resources, co-workers, co-clients, or superseded caregivers. She claims that providers shift between these various frames of reference according to the individual circumstances of each client/carer. She notes though that carers as clients or resources represent the predominant reality of community care (Twigg, 1992).

There are several forms of service provision that have as their primary objective support of informal carers. These include home, day and residential respite schemes, and carer support groups (Scottish Executive, 2006a).

Carers might also be indirectly supported by services that are aimed at the care recipient or when decisions relating to the care recipient take account of carers' circumstances (Twigg, 1992; Twigg and Atkin, 1994). Despite this provision though, it is becoming increasingly apparent that the link between carers' stress and the use of alternative sources of care is not straightforward (O'Connor, 1995; Burholt et al., 1997).

Use of services

Simply providing services does not ensure their use. Research indicates that relatively few carers use formal services (Taylor and Ford, 1994; PRTC, 1998b; McDonald, 1999; Curtice et al., 2002; Maher and Green, 2002; Scottish Executive, 2006a). In Taylor and Ford's (1994) study, three-quarters of carers were not in receipt of support services. In Curtice et al.'s (2002) study of intensive support packages for older people, just under half of carers in the community sample received some assistance from formal service providers. According to statistics from the General Household Survey (GHS), 77% of people whose carers lived in the same household received no regular visits from health and social care providers (Maher and Green, 2002). While the literature documents the issue and suggests that some carers (Evandrou, 1990; Taylor and Ford, 1994), and spouses in particular (George and Gwyther, 1990; Wenger, 1990; Parker, 1993; Howard, 2001), are reluctant to use formal services, it fails to explain it adequately.

Why are some carers reluctant or unable to accept available service support from formal providers? A few studies have examined this issue in relation to people with learning disabilities (Stalker et al., 1999; Grant, 2001), or ethnic minorities (Blakemore and Bonham, 1993; Boneham et al., 1997; Gunaratnam, 1997), or in relation to mental health services (Albert et al., 1998; Clarkson and McCrone, 1998): very few have looked at the issue of non-use among family carers of older people (O'Connor, 1995; Stearns and Butterworth, 2001). No published reviews of this theme exist, and even recent studies of services only touch briefly upon the topic (Twigg and Atkin, 1994; Nocon and Qureshi, 1996; Burholt et al., 1997; Brereton and Nolan, 2000), or concentrate on predisposing factors such as gender, age and disability rather than the reasons for non-use (Boniface and Denham, 1997).

Research examining service use seems to be concerned with evaluating the quality of services by measuring users' satisfaction levels (Langan et al., 1995; Ashworth et al., 1996; Clarke et al., 1999; Hardy et al., 1999;

Jarrett et al., 1999; Raynes et al., 2001). Studies of people's experiences of welfare services have consistently found high levels of expressed satisfaction among both service users (Allen et al., 1992; Wilson, 1995; Ashworth et al., 1996; McDonald, 1999) and carers (Mudge and Ratcliffe, 1995; Myers and McDonald, 1996; Ashworth and Baker, 2000). These findings make the issue of non-use more perplexing. If users and carers are on the whole satisfied with the services they receive, why do so few use them?

In some studies where respondents were apprehensive about receiving formal care services, their worries, based on their own and friends' experiences, related to poor standards of care and dissatisfaction with previously received services (Aronson, 1990; Grant et al., 1994; Stalker et al., 1999). Formal services have also been criticised on the grounds of inflexibility in terms of the types of tasks undertaken and the timing of services (Sinclair, 1990; Twigg and Atkin, 1994, Raynes et al., 2001). Other criticisms have focused on a lack of continuity of care (Simpson et al., 1995; Curtice et al., 2002), low levels of provision (Grant et al., 1994; Stalker et al., 1999), and communication problems between providers and service recipients (Simpson et al., 1995; O'Connor, 1995; Myers and McDonald, 1996; Boneham et al., 1997). These findings suggest that there might be a variety of reasons why individuals who need support from formal services do not utilise them.

Another common reason cited for under-use of services among older people in general, and carers in particular, is related to limited knowledge or awareness of services (Wright, 1986; Jutras and Veilleux, 1991; Sinclair, 1994; Schofield et al., 1998). This in turn is associated with the availability of information about services. Difficulty in finding out what is available is a recurring theme in research on services within the fields of community care and learning disabilities (Boniface and Denham, 1997; McDonald, 1999; Stalker et al., 1999). Lack of information or insufficient or inaccessible information is disabling and disempowering. Moreover, it has an adverse effect on carers' ability to establish what support is available and how to access it. Yet, carers do not like to ask for information; rather they want it to be freely available (Simpson et al., 1995; McDonald, 1999).

Simpson et al. (1995) suggest a reluctance to ask for information is possibly because of a perceived imbalance of power between the two groups concerned. From a sociological perspective, service providers are seen as powerful and knowledgeable, while carers are seen as powerless and unable to make themselves understood (Hugman, 1991; Simpson et al., 1995; Hogg, 1999; Twigg, 2000). The issue of communication and a lack of information is one of real frustration for carers as they have difficulty in coping with professional jargon and the aura of power (Hugman, 1991; Heyman, 1995; Simpson et al., 1995). Moreover, older people who have long experienced old-fashioned traditions may have an ingrained awe of professionals. They may also have fewer educational advantages than younger people;

advantages which would facilitate a freer exchange of information (Simpson et al., 1995; Twigg, 2000). However, other studies have noted that even with active recruitment, encouragement, and free access to services, nearly one-third of carers eligible for services do not use them (Caserta et al., 1987; Chapman, 1997). While the findings discussed above suggest that information, knowledge and accessibility are important factors accounting for service use, they do not adequately explain non-use by fully informed individuals.

In trying to understand non-use of services, some studies point to the importance of understanding an individual's history of involvement with service providers (Grant et al., 1994; O'Connor, 1995). In the course of Grant et al.'s (1994) study on how carers appraised service quality, respondents who expressed a reluctance to contact service providers were questioned further. Of those who expressed reluctance, just over half the carers said it was because they preferred to be self-reliant, 28% because of 'bad experiences' with providers in the past, 24% because they considered service providers to lack resources, and 17% because insufficient help had been received in the past. These reasons are unrelated to need, access, information or knowledge of services.

The widely held assumption within the literature that non-use is due to a lack of knowledge and awareness of available services has been shown to be an inadequate explanation. Moreover, this literature review reveals that few studies are concerned specifically with non-users of services (Eagles, 1987; Stalley, 1991; O'Connor, 1995). Clearly, there is scope for furthering our understanding of carers' reasons for not using formal services as a source of support.

Caregiving career

Caring has been likened to a career with a beginning, a discernible temporal direction and an end; stages which encompass 'markers' that highlight when carers may be more in need of, or more receptive to support (Montgomery and Kosloski, 2000). These markers are: performing tasks previously undertaken by others; self-definition as carer; giving personal care; seeking assistance and formal service use; considering nursing home placement; nursing home placement; and termination of care. While these markers are potentially useful, they are portrayed as developing sequentially and in a deterministic way which does not accord with the experiences of all carers. Moreover, this conceptualisation focuses on the practical aspects of caregiving and overlooks the more invisible but nonetheless important dimensions of caring, such as feelings of responsibility and the desire for control.

Others who have used the concept of a caregiving career to describe the transitions and role changes that carers experience over time have identified three broad phases to such a career (Aneshensel et al., 1995). These phases were: preparation for and acquisition of the caregiving role; enactment of caregiving; disengagement from caregiving.

Some authors have made more elaborate attempts to explore the sequential stages of the caregiving career. Wilson's (1989) work, for example, based on a small-scale study of twenty carers, describes an eight-stage model of care. These stages are: noticing; discounting or normalising; suspecting; search for explanations; recounting; taking it on; going through it; and turning it over. In a later study, Willoughby and Keating (1991) suggest a five-stage model comprising: emerging recognition; taking it on; gaining control; relinquishing control; and letting go. This model, however, being concerned primarily with admission to long-term care, focuses mainly on the processes of 'taking it on' and 'relinquishing control'.

In order to understand how caring changes over time, Keady and Nolan (1993, 1995) outline a longitudinal model of the key transition points in caregiving. This model is based on in-depth interviews with 58 dementia carers in contact with formal service providers. The six stages of this model are: building on the past; recognising the need; taking it on; working through it; reaching the end; and finally; a new beginning. Rather than concentrating on the beginning and ending of caregiving, this model explores each transition in the caregiving process. The authors contend that caregiving must be conceptualised in this way in order to develop effective, stage-specific service interventions (Keady and Nolan, 1993, 1995; Nolan et al., 1996).

While the temporal models outlined above have been derived from small-scale studies of service users, they are nonetheless valuable in encouraging caregiving to be conceptualised as a process rather than simply instrumental activities. However, these models have emerged from the literature on dementia, a degenerative condition with a recognised pathway, and so map carers' experiences in line with the condition's progress. They fail to address the temporal and dynamic nature of caring for older people without any cognitive impairment, people whose descent into frailty and increasing dependency is not assured.

The lack of temporal and longitudinal models of caring has been noted by a number of authors (Tamborelli, 1993; Thompson et al., 1993; Opie, 1994; Nolan et al., 1996). The majority of studies that do adopt a longitudinal design tend to be quantitative, descriptive research, which fails to capture the individualistic experiences of carers (Bauld et al., 2000a; Hutton and Hirst, 2001). What is needed is a detailed understanding of the way caring changes over time, in order that services can provide the appropriate support at the most appropriate time (Nolan et al., 2003).

Emerging from the study of hidden carers on which this book is based, are nine processes which taken together form a unique temporal model of caregiving. This builds on the earlier work of Nolan and Grant (1992), whose model was developed further in the field of dementia by Nolan et al. (1996). The model presented here, however, is derived from the experiences of carers of frail older people without dementia, who were at the start of the study non-users of services. The model, which proposes that caregiving can be conceptualised as nine stages in a caregiving career, lies at the heart of this book. These stages are as follows:

- dawning realisation;
- adopting the carer role;
- going it alone;
- gaining expertise;
- sinking or swimming;
- accessing services;
- carers as clients;
- continuation of caring;
- new horizons.

This model reflects the evolutionary process of family caregiving and although it is presented as being linear it is not experienced as such. Some stages overlap with each other, and the time taken to reach a specific stage varies depending on individual circumstances. Similarly, the time spent in any one stage varies and in some cases carers may bypass a particular stage altogether. If we conceptualise a caregiving career as having a trajectory with a beginning, a middle and an end, the phases of 'dawning realisation', 'adopting the carer role' and 'going it alone' occur at the beginning of carers' careers. These stages tend to overlap with each other and are evident in chapter 3, which describes carers' experiences at the start of their caregiving career. 'Dawning realisation' refers to the process by which carers gradually become aware that their relative requires care. 'Adopting the carer role' refers to carers' acceptance of the responsibility for providing care.

In chapter 4, the processes of 'going it alone', 'gaining expertise' and 'sinking and swimming' are evident. 'Going it alone' is intended to portray the stage when carers are unsupported by formal service provision. It underpins all the early stages of the model until 'accessing services'. The temporal model of care suggests that 'going it alone' is the stage in which carers are hidden from service providers, that it is only one of a number of stages that all caregivers go through, and that there are specific times in the caring career when carers are more receptive to service intervention.

'Gaining expertise' refers to the process whereby carers, who tended to be unprepared for their role, become competent and proficient in carrying out the tasks associated with caregiving. 'Sinking and swimming' captures the ebb and flow in carers' perceptions of whether they are coping or not with the demands of caring. These stages might arguably reflect the middle stages in carers' careers.

The process of 'sinking or swimming' overlaps with 'accessing services', 'carers as clients' and 'continuation of caring'. These are evident in chapter

5, which outlines how carers made the transition from being hidden carers unsupported by service providers to being visible and supported. 'Accessing services' refers to the complex process whereby carers try to access support. This is often prompted by carers experiencing a crisis of some sort which leads to them seeking help. By accepting support, carers tend to be perceived by service providers as 'clients', although, as we have seen in the previous chapter, current policy aims to address this view of carers.

The 'continuation of caring' stage illustrates how, once in receipt of support services, carers are able to continue caring even though service intervention generates its own difficulties and tensions. The stages of 'accessing services', 'carers as clients' and 'continuation of caring' represent the later stages of caring and are in some cases played out over a number of years. The book refers to but does not fully explore the final stage of 'new horizons', which is an important and under-researched area that needs further exploration.

As previously stated, current policy has been devised with the needs of carers already known to service providers in mind. If the experiences of hidden carers remain unexplored, then their needs will continue to be unmet. Moreover, if, as research has shown, carers are reluctant to utilise formal service provision, then policy will fail to meet its objectives. Policymakers need to ensure that services for carers are effective and accessible and will make a positive difference to their lives. This entails being aware of the needs of *all* carers and not just those already known to service providers.

CHAPTER 3

Experiences of Hidden Carers

According to statistics, 31,000 people a year in Scotland become carers (Carers Scotland, 2006), many of whom will remain hidden or invisible to service providers (Eley, 2003). The purpose of this chapter is to explore the experiences of these carers and the issues that are important to them. It presents insights into the early stages of caring that have been referred to as 'dawning realisation', 'adopting the carer role' and 'going it alone'. The chapter considers whether the experience of hidden carers differs from that of carers known to service providers and researchers. It begins by looking at how individuals become carers and why.

There appears to be an increasing awareness within policy and academic literature that the transition into a caring role is a crucial phase (Askham, 1998; Banks, 1999; Department of Health, 1999; Brereton and Nolan, 2000; Gillies, 2000). Linked to this is the notion of choice. The intention of policy as stated in recent documents is to 'support people who choose to become carers' (Department of Health, 1999; Scottish Executive, 2001a, 2006a, 2006b). But how many people actually choose to become carers?

Becoming a carer

> I had no choice in the matter. Not really, because there wasn't anybody else...I think I'm doing this because it's my duty, or I've been made to feel this is my duty. I don't know. I've got ambivalent feelings about that. (Mrs Gordon, 63-year-old carer)

The way in which a caring role was assumed had implications for the degree of choice that can be exercised. Essentially there were two main pathways to becoming a carer. Individuals became carers either by *default* or via a *positive pathway*. The key difference between these pathways was the degree to which the concept of choice was present. The positive pathway featured a degree of choice available to individuals who were free to exercise that choice and decide whether or not to accept the responsibility of looking after their relative. On the other hand, the default pathway featured a distinctive lack of choice.

Default pathway

For the majority of hidden carers entry to caring was 'by default'. This tended to be because they were already living with the person needing care and their willingness to assume the role was taken for granted. Thus they became carers 'by default' by virtue of their co-resident status, which reduced or removed the element of choice. The co-resident status of these carers was usually a pre-existing arrangement and not a consequence of the dependent person's need for care.

Individuals who became carers 'by default' tended to feel that they had no choice other than to accept the responsibility for care because they felt that 'there is no one else'. Spouse carers in particular expressed a feeling of having no choice that it was their duty and responsibility to care for their partner; they believed that to care was an inherent part of their marriage contract. This belief is perhaps because marriage in our society is regarded at an ideological level as the supreme caring relationship (Ungerson, 1987; Parker, 1993). Marriage vows, to which many spouses referred, reinforce the idea that one of the fundamental responsibilities of marriage is to care 'in sickness and in health'. Thus the care given by spouses was often seen as an extension of the love and support that is a mutual expectation of modern marriage. Wives and husbands were carers by default because they were simply fulfilling their ascribed role as spouses and to do otherwise would have perhaps undermined their relationship.

Sons and daughters also expressed feelings of having no choice but to care for their parents. Their accounts featured an underlying sense of duty and obligation to older parents. The majority of these caregiving relationships were based on love and affection, but others were not. Daughters were caring for parents while admitting that they had little or no affection for them. In the absence of other family members who were willing to provide care, these individuals were quite resentful of the position they found themselves in but felt, nonetheless, that they had no choice, that they were morally obliged to care for their ageing parents. These carers also expressed feelings of guilt for having no love or affection for their parents and it was this, along with a sense of duty, that motivated them to continue. Chappell (1990) claims it is only when a spouse has not been or is no longer available that children of an older person become the main carer. This was certainly true for sons and daughters who happened to live in the same household prior to the death of a spouse. For instance, Mrs Kearns and Mrs Gordon became carers by default following the death of a parent; they felt they had no choice but to care for their remaining parent simply because they were already living in the household when their services were required.

For the majority of hidden carers the default pathway into caring was a gradual process that took place over months or in some cases years. A slow deterioration in the health of the cared-for person was the most common reason why people began providing assistance. The increasing need for care was hardly noticeable at first. Only as the demands placed upon them took up more time did carers become aware of how much care they were providing.

> It was so gradual. You know I just started doing things for her and you never really noticed it and then — suddenly you realise that you're doing everything. Most of the time it is OK. You want to do it, but sometimes you just think, you know, why me? (Ms Peters, 47-year-old carer)

This gradual process was characterised by a steady increase in the amount of care given. As the cared-for person became more frail or immobile, the other partner in the household, be they spouse or daughter or son, increasingly undertook practical tasks and personal care.

Positive pathway

In contrast to the default pathway, the positive pathway was characterised by the presence of choice. This was the path taken by non-resident adult children who were free to exercise choice and who had to make a decision about the future care of their parent. Carers who felt that they had made a positive decision to care expressed fewer negative feelings about caring than those who felt they had had no choice. These carers did not feel as though pressure was being put upon them to look after their relatives. The realisation that they had a choice and that they were not being coerced into any particular course of action made a difference to their decision.

> I think because I had the option, I had the choice. That's what it was. I felt I had the choice, do I want to do it or do I not want to do it, and that felt good because you seem to feel that you're not in control of your life. (Mrs Cranston, 50-year-old carer)

The positive and default pathways were not always clearly defined; sometimes the boundaries between them were indistinct. There were some carers who do not 'fit' neatly into one category or the other. Some non-resident carers began giving care as the need arose, at a time when they believed that they had a choice in the matter. As time went on, though, and the task became more onerous, the longer they were involved in caring the harder it was for them to put a stop to their role. Their difficulty in drawing a line on their caring activities was often because of the close and affectionate relationship they enjoyed with the cared-for person.

Motivation

In assuming responsibility for caregiving people were motivated by affection, reciprocity or obligation. Although different motivations are discussed here as though they are separate entities, they are not mutually exclusive concepts. In reality the boundaries between them are hazy and overlapping and carers may be motivated by one or more factors. It cannot be said that carers who were motivated by reciprocity did not feel affection for the person they were caring for. Nor can it be said that carers motivated by affection did not feel a sense of obligation to their relative.

Carers who had a strong attachment to the person they were caring for were more likely to be motivated by affection rather than reciprocity or a sense of obligation. Their relationships tended to be close, with a strong emotional bond. Thus the majority of spouse carers, who tended to have strong, close relationships, were motivated by the love and affection they felt for their long-term partner. But sons, daughters and sisters were also motivated by affection for and attachment to their relative.

> He's my brother and I love him. It's as simple as that. (Mrs Ireland, 63-year-old carer)

Other carers were motivated by reciprocity. Reciprocity is defined as a social relationship between individuals in which there is a mutual exchange of goods or services that benefit both parties (Gouldner, 1973; George, 1986). According to Gouldner (1973), the norm of reciprocity decrees that people should help those who have helped them. It is a value that underpins human behaviour and exchanges within relationships (George, 1986).

Although the notion of reciprocity was not usually referred to or articulated directly by carers, good caregiving relationships were more likely to be based on the idea of an exchange of services. Mrs Welsh, for example, never forgot that her mother's support allowed her to escape from an abusive marriage and maintain her independence. When her mother's increasing frailty made caregiving more difficult, it was memories of past support and the notion of repaying a debt that motivated her caregiving. Her understanding of the reciprocal nature of family relationships was clear when she spoke about her reasons for looking after her mother. It was, as she said, 'payback time'.

In some caregiving relationships the notion of 'payback' or reciprocity was often very similar to notions of doing the right thing or duty. Spouse carers, especially, tended to regard caring for their partner as a natural part of their marriage, but they also saw it in some sense as a repayment for their partner having been a good husband or wife. Referring to the reciprocal nature of her relationship, Mrs Currie told how, when she was very ill many years before, her husband had nursed her at home for a number of months until she made a full recovery. She explained that caregiving was her responsibility because:

> Well after all, he's been my husband now for coming up to 60 years and I feel well — because he's been good to me. Who else would look after him? He's been good to me ... When I was very ill — I was at death's door years ago he was always there. He had to do more or less everything in the house ... He's not able to do anything now. (Mrs Currie, 83-year-old carer)

Caring allowed people to fulfil their sense of duty or obligation to another person. However, carers whose sense of obligation did not allow them to physically withdraw from caregiving did so emotionally. This was as true for spouses as it was for sons and daughters, whose sense of obligation often stemmed from their position in the family. If, for example, they were the eldest or the only daughter, or indeed if they were the youngest and fittest of their siblings, they were expected to take responsibility for caregiving. Mrs Bennet, for example, a recently retired woman looking after her 94-year-old mother, viewed caring as problematic and unrewarding. There were traces of bitterness in her words when she described what it was like to grow up in a household with strict parents who showed little affection towards their children:

> I don't love my mother. I see [caring] as my duty. She's never been a mother to me, although I am the eldest. She's never showed me any affection, or my brothers and sisters for that matter. She didn't criticise directly but everything that happened was wrong somehow.
> (Mrs Bennet, 67-year-old carer)

Many carers were motivated by a desire not to see their loved one end their days in long-term care, a reason with strong links to notions of familial obligations. As the health of an elderly parent or spouse deteriorated, carers often believed that the only realistic alternative was long-term care. This was taken to mean residential or nursing home care, which carers referred to as 'homes'. Carers held rather negative views of residential or nursing homes, usually doubting the quality of the care given.

Pathways to caring were precipitated by critical incidents such as a deterioration in the health of the cared-for person, the death of a spouse or parent, or an accident and subsequent discharge from hospital. The nature of the critical incident usually determined the pace with which individuals became carers. Becoming a carer varied in rapidity from gradual to very sudden. For those who felt that they had no choice, the decision-making process was almost non-existent. Some carers with a degree of choice made quick decisions followed by rapid action. For others the decision-making process could be slow and protracted while they considered the available options. Once the decision had finally been made, putting it into effect could take a matter of weeks to a few months. Thereafter, undertaking practical and personal care tended to be rapid.

Caring activities

The provision of personal and physical care was the defining feature of caregiving. Carers carried out tasks that people could not do for themselves and that have been described in detail by other studies (Lewis and Meredith, 1988; Parker, 1993; Twigg and Atkin, 1994; Nolan et al., 1996). The intention of this section is not to repeat these detailed descriptions. Rather it is to confirm that hidden carers carried out the full range of caregiving activities described as personal care (Scottish Executive, 2001a), and that they did so without support from service providers. They were in effect 'going it alone'. These caregiving activities included personal care such as bathing, assistance with dressing, help with surgical appliances, help to get up and go to bed, and dealing with the consequences of poor mobility. It also included help with toileting, catheter care, skin care, medication, application of cream and lotions, simple dressings, oxygen therapy, incontinence laundry, bed changing, household chores and food preparation.

Personal care defined as 'self-care' or the things that an adult would normally do for themselves (Twigg, 2000: 44) seemed to be more problematic than care of a physical or practical nature. While carers tended to accept that providing care of that nature was part of their role, this aspect of caregiving caused a mixture of emotions ranging from embarrassment to distress and disgust.

For the majority of spouse carers, providing personal care for their partner was not particularly problematic. However, some older spouse carers said that initially they found it embarrassing to perform intimate care for their partner. Carers tended to use humour to lighten the situation and detract from their feelings of awkwardness and embarrassment. Mrs Yuill, for example, described how when her husband was in hospital she worried about having to wash and dress him when he came home:

> When he came out at first I thought how am I going to manage — he'll be embarrassed, I'll be embarrassed and I worried about that. Although we're not really embarrassed now. I try to make it fun. When I put him into bed at night I have to help him and I'll say I'll bloody choke you and he just laughs because he knows I'm not going to choke him. I says I've got you at my mercy now. So I try to make light of it. I try to laugh and make it fun. (Mrs Yuill, 75-year-old carer)

Distress at having to perform personal and intimate care was greater among sons and daughters, particularly if they were caring for a parent of the opposite sex. While accepting that intimate care was generally a normal part of caregiving, sons and daughters expressed not just acute embarrassment or discomfort but also distaste and revulsion at the thought of having to help their parent with personal and intimate care. On the whole, the difficulty arose not from the type of care required but rather from the gender of the care recipient. Mrs Thompson, for example, only bathed her father during occasional periods of poor health when he tended to become incontinent and needed more frequent help with personal hygiene. While she did not regard herself as a 'prude', neither did she feel it was proper for her to bathe her father. She conceded that her reactions would probably be different if her mother needed the same type of care. She explained that she had bathed her father 'at the beginning' when he was quite ill and she believed that he was only going to live for a few weeks. Now that death was no longer imminent she found it increasingly difficult to undertake personal care. The intimate and private nature of these tasks meant that, like other carers in a similar situation, Mrs Thompson resolved the problem by turning to her family for help. She was fortunate that her sons were more than happy to regularly undertake the personal care their grandfather required:

> When's he's having a bath or a wash my sons attend to that for me. When he was just home from hospital I could do it then. I did everything for him because at that time it was like a case of well this is only going to be for a few weeks. Now when it's a permanency, well my sons take over, they see to him. (Mrs Thompson, 41-year-old carer)

Cross-sex caring also presented difficulties for male carers. Mr Clark, for example, looked after his 83 year-old mother who suffered from slight urinary incontinence. While he was extremely reluctant to assist her to wash and bathe, he recognised that she increasingly needed more assistance with personal hygiene. At the time of the first interview his mother's incontinence did not present too much of a problem. He simply reminded her to wash properly and ensured that clean underwear was available for her every morning. As time went on, though, her increasing frailty and poor eyesight made it more difficult for her to keep herself clean. She steadfastly refused to accept help from her son, who admitted that he would be too embarrassed to bathe and toilet his mother.

In having to perform personal care, sons and daughters seemed to be constrained by the normative expectations concerning the child-parent relationship. According to Twigg and Atkin (1993, 1994), in the relationship between children and their parents there are greater expectations of privacy, autonomy and separation than in a marriage relationship. In other words, children are generally expected to receive care from their parents rather than give it, and to leave home and lead independent, separate lives. So what was acceptable for a parent to do for a child differed from what children might be expected to do for their parent. Thus, because carrying out personal and intimate care was less likely to be seen as a natural part of a child-parent relationship, it created difficulties for some adult child carers (Atkin, 1992).

While no caregiving situation was completely free of difficulties, carers who had a strong and emotionally close relationship with the cared-for person were more likely to perceive caring as unproblematic. In contrast, carers who had a fragile and emotionally distant relationship with the person being cared for were more likely to view caring as difficult and beset with problems. Problematic caregiving relationships were often characterised by conflict and tension, which was often related to issues of control.

Control of caregiving

This section explores how control of caregiving situations was established and maintained. Caregiving has been acknowledged as a relationship in which either one or the other of the parties has more control (Twigg, 2000; Orme, 2001). Previous research on control and power within caregiving has focused on the relationship between service providers and service users and carers (Twigg and Atkin, 1994; Twigg, 2000). Here the focus is on the relationship between the carer and care recipient.

Control, defined as the ability to exercise power in order to direct or manage the caring situation, was a particularly important issue for hidden carers. Power, the tool used to achieve and maintain control, can be defined as domination, legitimate authority, an act of will or the probability that a person in a relationship would be able to carry out his or her own will in the pursuit of goals regardless of resistance (Lukes, 1987).

Control of the caregiving situation was established and maintained through ownership of material resources such as money or the house where care was being delivered. A widely held belief among carers was that home ownership conferred a degree of authority that enabled the homeowner to control the situation. Carers who had brought their older relative to live with them believed that because caring was taking place in their house, they had the authority to make rules and establish boundaries. They found it relatively easy to exercise power and establish their authority. Carers believed that whoever owned the home had the authority to establish 'ground rules' and 'call the tune':

> I've always said that as a carer, they stay with *me*. I do not stay with them. There's a subtle difference in that kind of thing. It makes a difference if you start that way. If someone is living with you, you've got to have a set of ground rules to start with and if things get worse or alter, you have to change the rules. I think it makes a difference because it means that you can still have your own life. (Mrs Smith, 50-year-old carer)

On the other hand, carers who chose to move into their parent's house found it difficult to establish their authority in someone else's home. Mr Clark's mother tried to control the situation by the straightforward assumption of parental authority:

> Mum suggested that I come and live with her. I felt that because we got on well together coupled with the fact that she needed more care, that it would work out OK. But it's been a disaster. It's her home so I'm conscious of that and I can't make any rules. I wish I had never moved. (Mr Clark, 50-year-old carer)

Mr Clark did not appreciate that his mother's attitude might change once he had moved in with her. That the house was hers was a fact she frequently reminded him of. Mr Clark came to the realisation that when his mother had stayed in his home, she reacted in a different way. She acted and was treated like a guest who made few demands on her host. In her own home, however, she became more assertive and demanding, reverting perhaps to the previous parent-child relationship. She made sure that her son knew that he was there on her terms and that it was she who was firmly in control of the situation. For Mr Clark, moving into his mother's home led to a loss of power, independence and autonomy. The relationship had changed from one of dependence to one of interdependence.

The issue of home ownership was also important for non-resident carers. Some anticipated the effect that residency might have on the balance of power. Mrs Welsh, for instance, was adamant that she would not give up her home to live with her 93-year-old mother, but she felt that it was expected of her. She believed that if she gave up her own home she would lose her autonomy and independence. She expressed her fear that if she moved in she would constantly be at her mother's 'beck and call'. While she expressed feelings of guilt at not living with her mother, she recognised her own need for independence and her own physical space:

> I'll not give up my house and go and stay with her. She's still got a bit of independence and so have I. I don't want to be always at her beck and call. You just feel sometimes you should, but I couldn't give up my own home ... but it lurks at the back of my mind. (Mrs Welsh, 62-year-old carer)

Another way of exercising power was by having control of financial resources. In Mr Brown's case, his father, the cared-for person, was never consulted about any issues even when they directly affected him, nor was he aware how much money he was paid in pensions or how it was spent. Mr Brown had brought his father to live with him. He had full control of his father's income and spent it as he saw fit, although any goods bought with his father's money usually benefited both men. While Mr Brown talked in terms of 'we', his father was not in a position either to decide how to spend his money or on what it was spent. Mr Brown justified his control of joint finances by viewing it as a 'family thing' and implying that he would eventually inherit the money anyway. Moreover, despite being eager earlier in the interview to establish his ownership of the home, when it came to finances Mr Brown was keen for the house to be viewed as 'ours':

> Basically his money is my money is the way we look at it. I mean it's a kind of family thing, you know. He's got the money and he'll just say you can't take it with you. The rest of my family, my mother and brother don't want to know. They don't want money

off him. So whatever money is left I get and I spend on me or on the house, our house. That's how we can afford to renovate the flat. The money is there ... and it benefits him as much as it benefits me. Technically it was his money but he can't take it with him and when he dies I get it anyway. So I am as well spending it as I get it. That's the way I look at it. (Mr Brown, 40-year-old carer)

Despite being dependent on a carer for practical care, ownership of financial resources could give care recipients power that was deployed when it came to making decisions. An example of this was the case of Mr Paul, whose 74-year-old wife, the care recipient, controlled the household finances and attempted to use this to manipulate her husband. Mr Paul's wife, being ten years older than her spouse, was in receipt of a generous occupational pension as well as a state pension. He, on the other hand, having been made redundant just as his wife's need for care increased, had never sought another job and was dependent on state benefits. His only source of income was the Carers Allowance. Since his wife had the greater income Mr Paul was dependent on her financially. This meant that she had to give him money with which to buy food and anything else that was required.

Mrs Paul's ownership of financial resources gave her power that she deployed when it came to making decisions about issues such as holidays and childminding and even where they would live. When the local council made them an offer of another house in a different area, Mrs Paul decided that they should accept it despite her husband's objections. She would decide where and when they would have a holiday and would agree to babysit for her daughter without consulting her husband. Yet he was the one who had to take care of the children because his wife's condition precluded her from doing so.

This finding of a link between control of finances and decision-making is similar to that of other studies. For example, in Pahl's (1989) study of power within marriage, it was found that power lay with whoever controlled the money and those who controlled the finances had greater power in decision-making. In Pahl's study it was usually males rather than females that controlled the money and therefore had greater power in decision-making, but the principle remains the same. Decision-making was therefore another way in which control was maintained in caregiving relationships.

Irrespective of who had control of material resources, the competing interests of the carer and the cared-for, and their attempts to control the caregiving situation, generated conflict. Despite appearing powerless, there were instances of care recipients who challenged their carer's authority by either refusing to comply with their decisions or by making their opposition known. This resistance often resulted in conflict or a battle of wills between the carer and the cared-for person. The most striking example of a relationship in which the cared-for person exercised more power and control over decision-making than the carer was that of Mrs Watson and her father.

Mrs Watson had moved into the family home to care for her father after the death of her mother. That the move had not been entirely successful she put down to her father's possessive and domineering nature. Although she actually owned half the house, she still regarded it as belonging to her father. Moreover, she believed that home ownership conferred certain rights, which allowed her father to exercise power over her and her family. She felt that he was constantly trying to manipulate and control her life. The television remote control had become a symbol of the power struggle going on. Mrs Watson's father exercised the authority vested in him by ownership of the house by deciding what television programmes were watched. He managed this by ensuring that the television remote control was always by his side. When Mrs Watson or her husband seemed interested in a particular programme he would switch channels without warning, maintaining that he could watch what he wanted because it was 'his house, his furniture, his telly, his remote control'. This action was always guaranteed to cause an argument.

Control of the television seemed to symbolise Mrs Watson's father's attempts to control his household and his life. The extent to which the care recipient in this case controlled the situation was unusual but was apparently made possible by his belligerent and forceful personality which overshadowed that of his daughter. By opposing her wishes, Mrs Watson's father seemed to successfully wield power and hence control over his daughter.

In relationships characterised by conflict, a tactic used by some carers to redress the balance of power was the use of threats. Mrs Beaton used threats as a means by which to limit her father's power and control his demanding and difficult behaviour. At the first stage of the study, Mrs Beaton's father seemed to be firmly in control of the situation in that his wishes dominated the activities of the entire household. However, by the third and final interview she had discovered that the threat of institutionalisation was enough to modify his behaviour. Between interviews Mrs Beaton's father had been hospitalised on four occasions. On the last occasion plans were made, without consultation, for him to be admitted to long-term care. When she discovered this, Mrs Beaton refused to allow her father's transfer to long-stay care to proceed. While she felt that her relationship with her father, not good to begin with, would improve if they lived apart, she felt she could not agree to his admission to a care home. That she had prevented him from going into a home was subsequently used as a threat by Mrs Beaton to ensure her father's good behaviour. She warned him that she could easily arrange his admission by simply contacting the GP. The passage below illustrates the changes in Mrs Beaton's approach to caring and how she was now more in control of the situation than previously. She explained how her father tried to revert to his old ways after he came home from hospital and how she dealt with his behaviour. Feelings of guilt rather than affection compelled her to refuse the offer of long-term care:

Although I say I don't care where he's going, at the same time, I do care. So while at times he could go to hell as far as I'm concerned, at the same time I don't want to see him going into a home ... I am harder with him. I have threatened him. I told him he would go back into hospital if he started again. He said, 'I promise I'll no start again'. I was ready to smother him. He was acting the pig again. It's as if he's saying, 'I'm going to see how far I can push her'. I told him that it could be taken out of his hands. I said, 'when you were in hospital, they were going to send you away, and they never even told you'. He knows that it just takes one word from me and he's off. My doctor said to me, just say the word and we'll get him in somewhere. (Mrs Beaton, 68-year-old carer)

The threat of long-term care seemed to be effective in that Mrs Beaton's father had since modified his behaviour, although his acquiescence may have been due in part to his increasing frailty. Nonetheless, Mrs Beaton seemed to have gained the upper hand by establishing a new routine and a set of rules by which her father had to abide. This new regime included her father retiring to his own bedroom earlier in the evening. There he could watch his own television while his daughter and her family were free to watch whatever they wanted in the sitting room. By her own admission Mrs Beaton was becoming 'harder with him'.

The accounts of the experience of caring discussed above show how in caregiving relationships power was exercised in order to encourage one person to conform to what the other regarded as acceptable behaviour. Threats were used by one person in an attempt to both force the other to comply with these unwritten rules of behaviour and to redress the power imbalance in the relationship. The assumption of parental authority combined with home ownership made it very difficult for carers to view the house as *their* home. Consequently, they found it much more difficult to be assertive and were unable to establish rules of the relationship. Achieving control seemed to be related to carers' perceptions of stress and coping which are explored in the next chapter.

In many respects the experiences of hidden carers mirror those of carers known to service providers and researchers. For example, the ways in which they become carers and take on the role is the same. The literature suggests that many of them 'drift' (Lewis and Meredith, 1988) or 'slip' into their caring role, with the transition from non-carer to carer being 'imperceptible' (Murphy et al., 1997; Schofield et al., 1998). In the case of co-resident carers in particular, it is a continuation of a relationship where the level of dependency had grown progressively. In other situations, the process of becoming a carer happens almost instantaneously when, for example, an older person suffers from a sudden and unexpected accident or illness (Qureshi and Walker, 1989; Nolan et al., 1996; Brereton and Nolan, 2000). Moreover, a synthesis of the literature suggests that the factors which motivate carers, namely a sense of obligation, attachment and reciprocity (Parker, 1993; Orme, 2001; Nolan et al., 2003) are the same as those identified here.

There are very few studies which have examined in any depth the way in which control and issues of power in relationships are played out by carers and care recipients. Those that have suggest that, when each party is sensitive to the needs of the other, the relationship is likely to be positive (Cox and Dooley, 1996) rather than angry, demanding or abusive (Nolan, 1993). These studies, however, make no mention of carers' desire or need for control.

CHAPTER 4

Coping with Caregiving

This chapter explores how carers cope with caregiving. It begins by considering the causes of stress and the coping strategies and resources utilised by carers. It will discuss the role played by the outcomes of caring, before concluding with a description of certain temporal aspects of stress and caring. This chapter illustrates the processes of 'going it alone', 'gaining expertise' and 'sinking and swimming'.

The majority of carers in the present study said that caring was stressful and that stress increased over time. This perception seemed to be unrelated to either the stability or the quality of the caregiving situation or to the age of the carer. Stress was caused by the provision of personal and intimate care, other direct activities of care such as the behaviour of the cared-for person, tiredness, and having to negotiate with government and welfare agencies. Less visible activities such as the constant monitoring, supervision and planning were also reported as being sources of stress.

Stress seemed to have a cumulative effect on carers and was related to the way in which problems evolved and developed. Over time one source of stress such as the cared-for person's incontinence tended to generate others stressors such as broken sleep and tiredness. For a few carers, unremitting chronic stress seemed to lead to anxiety and depression.

The main coping strategies used by hidden carers were problem-solving and practical solutions, and cognitive and behavioural responses. Problem-solving and practical solutions include measures such as the use of routines (72%), talking over problems (81%), planning in advance (77%), getting information (67%) and establishing priorities and concentrating on them (91%). Mrs Gordon, for example, was rapidly approaching retirement and initially she dreaded the prospect of being with her father all day every day. But she eventually adopted a positive proactive approach by planning for her retirement, by introducing a new routine and by making her father do more for himself. She also described how she was able to 'switch off', a strategy frequently used by carers:

> I'm coping OK. I had got to the stage where I couldn't cope. Now I would say that I was coping better. I don't know if it's because I'm planning ahead and I've not allowed myself to think, 'Oh my

God, this is just going to get worse', which I used to do. Because I wasn't planning I wasn't looking for a way out. All I could see was doom and gloom ... I think because I am either consciously or subconsciously saying, 'No, it won't be how I'd like things to be in my life but I'm going to find ways of making it a bit better.' That has made things easier, and I don't stand for any of his nonsense now. We've got a routine now and we stick to that ... I find it easier now to switch off from him. And I think I cope great now. (Mrs Gordon, 63-year-old carer)

Mrs Gordon's account suggests that she used both problem-solving strategies and cognitive responses. She recognised that the problem was not going to disappear and so she changed the way in which she viewed it. While problem-solving strategies have been found to be the most effective method of coping (Boss, 1993), changing a perception of the cause of stress seemed to be equally useful.

Changing a perception of the cause of stress was among strategies based on cognitive responses. These responses encompassed such other measures as taking things a day at a time (100%), just getting on with it (86%), using humour (77%), drawing on religious beliefs (43%), counting your blessings, acceptance or minimising problems. Mrs Macrae, for example, who looked after her 93-year-old mother, said that her ability to cope 'varies depending on the situation'. She coped by reframing the problem and explained that:

I don't think about things being a problem because if I do — that's when it becomes too much and it gets on top of you and you just go under. No. I think of it as situations that have just got to be dealt with. That's the way I look at it. (Mrs Macrae, 63-year-old carer)

This seemed to be a practical and pragmatic approach to caring but it was underpinned by worry about the future. Carers said they were afraid to look too far into the future. If they did it caused them to worry and become anxious about their situation. They coped with this by:

Taking each day as it comes. I don't like thinking that in ten years' time she could still be here with me and I'll still be doing this and I'd still be ... No, because then it would bring me down. I just take it as it comes. (Mr Clark, 50-year-old carer)

Behavioural responses to coping were essentially efforts to deal with the *results* of stress. These strategies were activities that refocused the carer's mind, even if only for a short time. They included listening to music, reading, painting, even fighting or crying and taking drugs or alcohol. The majority of carers (91%) said that one way of dealing with the demands of caring was to take their mind off things by reading, or watching TV. Many carers (62%) said they tried to cheer themselves up by eating, drinking, smoking or the like. Just over half (52%) said they coped by having a good cry. Others used music as an escape from the stress of caring. Listening to music was an effective strategy because it involved either moving to another room or using headphones. Either way, by concentrating on their music, carers were able to emotionally distance themselves from the care recipient, if only for a short time:

> When it's all getting on top of me I put my music on or I have a wee cry. Sometimes I have a cry — in private. When there's no one about and when he's in bed. (Mrs Smith, 75-year-old carer)

The coping behaviours of hidden carers were similar to those described by other research. Carers' coping behaviour involved efforts to either change or alleviate a difficult situation, to alter or reduce perceived threats and to manage the symptoms of stress arising from the situation (Pearlin et al., 1990, 2001). Coping efforts can be enhanced or hindered by carers' access to coping resources (Pearlin, 1991). But what coping resources did hidden carers have access to and in what way, if any, did they support carers' attempts to cope?

Coping resources

The efficacy of coping strategies was enhanced by access to other coping resources such as social support and adequate accommodation. Many hidden carers tended to have small support networks and caring was rarely shared with other family members. Indeed some carers preferred to have sole responsibility for caregiving. They felt that the less involved their relatives were the less likelihood of disagreements within the family. This lack of support was often explained by the fact that the family had more important commitments. Mr Paul, for example, said that:

> They've either got full-time jobs or they've got children to look after. (Mr Paul, 63-year-old carer)

Appropriate accommodation also facilitated caregiving, while inappropriate living arrangements made it more difficult and could deter the independence of the care recipient. Mrs Black, for example, looked after her mother, who was incontinent. Their toilet was accessed by a short flight of stairs and because her mother had mobility problems she found it difficult to negotiate the stairs and was reluctant to attempt them herself. A friend had given her a commode but it was unsightly and embarrassing to use in the sitting room and it needed to be emptied. Other carers who lived in appropriate accommodation had made attempts to overcome problems with the use of aids and adaptations. Simple pieces of equipment such as strategically placed handrails, commodes and bathing aids made a considerable difference to the lives of both carers and care recipients by affording care recipients more independence and reducing the demands on carers' time. Another way in which accommodation was used as a coping resource was in the creation of personal space. Carers used the physical arrangements of the house as a means of achieving space for themselves. For example, many carers had created bed-sitting rooms for the care recipient, who was subsequently confined to one room while the family ate and socialised in another. If space allowed, some carers had literally divided the house into two apartments with communal use of the kitchen and bathroom. For example, Mrs Gordon and her father had their own sitting rooms and bedrooms but shared the kitchen, dining room and bathroom. Mrs Gordon valued having her own sitting room; it was a place of sanctuary that afforded her privacy and where she was unlikely to be disturbed. Some carers found it difficult to distance themselves emotionally when they could not get away physically, and said that it was more difficult to cope as time went on.

In the cases outlined above, co-resident carers had used their accommodation as a coping resource. Non-resident carers did not seem to experience the same feelings of frustration and claustrophobia caused by inadequate accommodation as co-resident carers did. By maintaining their own homes rather than forming a combined household, non-resident carers were able to create a physical separation from their caregiving activities. This physical separation seemed to make it easier for them to maintain an emotional distance. Thus accommodation, in that it either eased or obstructed carers' efforts, was an important coping resource.

Whether caregiving was perceived as being positive or negative also seemed to play an important role in carers' ability to cope. Carers who perceived themselves to be coping well were more likely to report the existence of positive outcomes.

Positive outcomes of caregiving

Positive outcomes refer to the consequences of caregiving from which carers derived a reward or a sense of satisfaction. Carers who felt that they were coping were more likely to report a greater number of positive outcomes. Positive outcomes arose from carers' ability to either protect the cared-for person from some negatively perceived event or to promote positive consequences. In other words, if caregiving was perceived as a satisfying experience, carers seemed to cope better. While this suggests that there is a link between positive outcomes and carers' ability to cope, the dynamics of this association are unclear.

Positive outcomes reported by carers included getting pleasure from seeing the care recipient happy — clean, comfortable, well turned out (95%) — and being able to maintain their dignity (91%). Other positive outcomes were an improvement in the care recipient's condition that had been contrary to medical opinion (86%) and the knowledge that they had done their best (86%). For the majority of carers (91%) in the present study, the fact that they were able to keep the person they cared about out of institutional care was a positive outcome. Carers tended to hold negative perceptions of both the quality of care and the standard of accommodation available in institutional care. While some based their perceptions on personal experience, others tended to rely instead on anecdotal evidence and hearsay.

For others, a positive outcome was that caring provided a purpose in life that they had previously lacked (47%) and also led to the development of new skills (38%) and the chance to widen interests and contacts (33%). These carers tended to be either unemployed or people whose children had grown up and left home. Caring provided their day with a structure and a purpose that had been lacking, as well as widening their interests. The development of new skills and interests was sometimes encouraged by attendance at painting, pottery and computing classes held in local community centres.

In contrast to carers who felt they were coping, others whose perception was that they were not coping were more likely to experience negative outcomes. These outcomes tended to increase carers' feelings of stress and were accompanied by expressions of negative emotions. The most consequential negative outcome was the restrictions that caring placed on carers' lives in general and social activities in particular. Restrictions on carers' lives often led to the loss of friends, social isolation and loneliness. Carers (67%) tended to feel that they did not have enough time for themselves, and 57% felt that they could not see their friends as often as they would like, have a break or take a holiday. Some expressed the view that caring had 'taken over' their lives and that looking after an older person was different from looking after children because few people were prepared to 'babysit' for an adult. Mrs Thompson, for example, believed that the restrictions on her life, the loss of friends and the ensuing isolation and loneliness were an inevitable part of caring. Referring to it as 'the caring syndrome', she explained that:

> If you take over the care of another person, you take over their life and they in turn overtake your life because your life is now, you don't exist any more. You really don't exist. Your friends that used to be your friends don't come. Your true friends get fed up with you saying no, you can't come out and then eventually the phone calls don't come. And it's not their fault. It's just a fact. It's one of the things that happen. You're just a carer. It's just the 'caring syndrome'. (Mrs Thompson, 40-year-old carer)

This account illustrates how some carers suffer from restrictions when the limits placed on the care recipient also affect their own lives. Restrictedness, according to Twigg and Atkin (1994), not only refers to the degree to which carers are unable to leave the cared-for person but it also encompasses the wider ways caring constrains and limits carers' activities. They suggest that restrictedness is central to carers' lives and as such poses a problem for all carers (Twigg and Atkin, 1994). This finding, though, is not consistent with those of this study, in which restrictedness was a problem for some but certainly not for all carers.

Some carers, usually those who said they were coping, refused to allow their caring responsibilities to restrict their social life. For them it was not so much the practical aspects of caring that restricted them, as a general worry about what might happen in their absence. Although in many of these cases there was no objective reason why the care recipient could not be left, carers tended to worry when they were left unsupervised. Mr Brown, for example, managed his feelings of restriction by devising an unusual way of checking up on his father's activities. By installing video cameras in strategic positions in the house, Mr Brown was able to monitor his father's movements. He discovered that his father's habits were fairly predictable in that he would make a trip to the toilet every time a commercial break came on the television. By using these 'big brother' tactics he was able to leave his father alone in the house feeling certain that nothing untoward would happen in his absence. Mr Brown subsequently used this means of surveillance on a regular basis whether he was in or out of the house. Although this measure seems a bit extreme, it was utilised in an attempt to overcome any restrictions caring placed on Mr Brown's social life.

Another negative outcome, described by 76% of carers, was that caregiving created demands that competed with other family responsibilities and that it put a strain on family relationships. Some carers felt that they were unable to devote enough time to other family members such as husband and children, and that caregiving was a threat to their marriage. This was a particular problem for younger married carers who were looking after a parent. The demands made on them by their husband and older parent were considerable and difficult to reconcile, and at times generated a great deal of tension. Some found that their husband complained about the amount of their time that was taken up with caregiving. In a few cases this seemed to cause conflict and jealously between the carer's partner and their parent who seemed to compete for attention.

Carers with young children were particularly resentful of the time spent with the care recipient; time which they believed should have been 'family time'. The stress that Mrs Kearns experienced seem to increase as both her mother and her children grew older and her husband became more resentful of the amount of time she devoted to caring. She admitted that at times she felt like 'piggy in the middle' and didn't seem able to please anybody. At the time of the second and third interviews Mrs Kearns was being treated for clinical depression which she attributed to the stress of caregiving. She explained that:

Each year she gets frailer and frailer and she can do less for herself. You feel that life's passing you by. The kids are getting bigger and there is so much you want to do with them and you don't get the chance. I think [caring] affects all the family because sometimes the girls will say something and you have to say we can't because we've got to do this or that for Granny. It's very difficult. My husband complains that I do too much for my mother. We've had a lot of rows and talked about splitting up. It's stressful because you have to try and split your time between so many people. I'm at everybody beck and call. I find that trying to get the time for the girls the less I give to [my mother]. (Mrs Kearns, 36-year-old carer)

Balancing the demands of a family was very difficult for carers. The tension within their marriage added to their experiences of physical and mental stress. The outcomes of caregiving seem to play an important role in carers' ability to cope; this finding is consistent with those of others such as Motenko (1989) and Nolan et al. (1996).

Temporal aspects of stress and coping

Stress and coping are processes that must be understood in context and over time. Analysis of the longitudinal data has highlighted the temporal and dynamic nature of caring by revealing three concurrent and inextricably linked processes associated with the development of stress and coping. One process was that carers' stress increased with the passage of time. The second was the development of expertise over time, whereby carers became increasingly skilled in the tasks and management of caregiving. The third process was the occurrence of crises in coping that sometimes marked a watershed in carers' careers. These processes did not necessarily precede or follow each other in a deterministic way, but rather they seemed to occur simultaneously. The time within which these processes took place varied enormously from a matter of months to years.

Increasing stress

The first discernable process was increasing levels of stress. The most common pattern among hidden carers was that, contrary to popular belief (Kahana and Young, 1990), caring was not perceived as being particularly stressful at the beginning. It was only as the time spent caring lengthened that perceptions changed. The time taken for carers' perceptions to change varied and seemed to be unrelated to the pathway by which individuals became carers or to the nature of the caregiving relationship. Mrs Duncan, for example, found at the start of her caregiving that it was 'far less stressful than living and working in London'. Six months later her views were beginning to change and she said that the 'novelty of not working has worn off. I feel I have no goals in life. I'm just going from day to day'. A year later there were few traces of the optimistic and capable woman who had had been interviewed previously. She cried throughout the third interview and admitted candidly that caring was 'very stressful'. She expressed regret at her decision to become a carer and about her loss of freedom. Although her mother's condition had not deteriorated, Mrs Duncan felt increasingly trapped and worn down by the constant responsibility of caring.

For other carers, the length of time spent caring did not seem to have any relation to their perception of stress. Some who had been caring for a number of years did not perceive it to be stressful and presumably that is why they had managed to continue caring for all that time. Mrs Currie, for example, who had been a carer for twenty years, said that caring was frustrating rather than stressful. Carers such as Mrs Currie were unusual in that unlike the others they did not experience caring as becoming increasingly stressful, yet their circumstances were broadly similar. For most of these carers, their present role was not their first experience of caring. This prior experience seemed to provide them with a degree of expertise that other carers lacked.

Development of expertise

The development of expertise was the second discernible process. Changes seemed to take place in carers' ability to cope over time. They appeared to develop a degree of expertise that led to an increase in confidence in their own abilities, and by the time of the final interview they reported that they were coping better than previously. Carers' accounts suggest that after a period of adjustment some adapted to and accepted their role. Having cared for her brother for six years, Mrs Ireland's view was that:

It's just a case of saying, well this is it. I don't think it gets easier but I think you become accustomed to it. I think you have to adapt or sink. I'm so used to it now. (Mrs Ireland, 63-year-old carer)

Practical experience of caregiving seemed to encourage the use of an increasing number of coping strategies. Through a process of trial and error, carers were able to determine what worked best and what was a waste of time. For example, some carers developed the ability to distance themselves emotionally from the situation. Mrs Kearns, for instance, said that when her mother got annoyed or upset with her she treated her like a child and 'let it all go over my head now'. Others reported that they were much more assertive and were now placing limits on their caregiving activities.

Evidence from the present study suggests that carers gain some degree of expertise similar to that described by Eraut (1994) in relation to professionals. Eraut's model sees the acquisition of expertise as a pathway from competence to proficiency and ultimately to expertise. He claims that normal or novice behaviour is characterised by an ability to carry out routine procedures. Competency is marked not only by an ability to carry out these procedures while under pressure but also to recognise and discriminate between the features of situations and plan accordingly. Proficiency marks the development of a different approach in that behaviour becomes semi-automatic rather than merely routine, situations are assessed and understood more comprehensively, and any abnormalities are noted and attended to quickly.

Eraut's pathway deems that expertise is acquired through practical experience rather than knowledge. He claims that there has been a shift away from the belief that professional practice is informed mainly by theoretical knowledge towards the realisation that in fact much of what happens emerges from experience. Family carers are similar to professionals in that they develop expertise through experience and their intimate knowledge of the situation. Although carers do not have any formal training in which rules and practical skills are introduced, they are similar to professionals in that expertise can only begin to develop when skills are practised and refined in real-life situations. Carers developed their skills mainly by a process of trial and error but their intimate knowledge of the care recipient and their experience allowed them to select the most appropriate way of dealing with stressful incidents. In the present study carer expertise was acquired by experience; it tended to be intuitive and was based on a skilled management of the situation.

The two processes described above present an apparent paradox whereby the majority of carers who said that caring became increasingly stressful seemed to be the same people who perceived themselves as coping better. One possible explanation for this paradox may lie in the crises that carers experience.

Periodic crises

An experience common to the majority of carers was of a crisis in coping followed by a period of appraisal and sometimes a change in mindset. During the crisis, carers were unable to maintain a reasonable emotional balance and negative feelings aroused by their situation were expressed. Crises were usually related directly to the caregiving situation, although external events added to the tension and to carers' sense of helplessness. The typical pattern was of a period of stability followed by a series of minor problems, each one dealt with in the way the carer thought most appropriate. Each problem, irrespective of its magnitude, increased the strain on the carer, especially if it was not resolved satisfactorily. The cumulative effect of strain seemed to result in 'carer overload'. This occurred when carers felt they 'had had enough' or were at 'breaking point' and could not continue to look after the care recipient.

The catalyst for a crisis appeared to be the cumulative effect of a number of stressful events. Incidents such as deterioration in the carer's or care recipient's health, increasing anger or resentment, and sometimes conflict with other members of the family contributed to carers' perceived inability to cope. Some carers also perceived caregiving as posing a threat to their marriage or to their own health. When asked how they had coped with crises in their lives, carers gave responses that were broadly similar, in that they all used verbal and written communication as a coping strategy. While some like Mrs Smith wrote in a diary, others talked to trusted confidantes and GPs about it. Vocalising or writing about how they felt helped carers to clarify their thoughts, their feelings and the options available to them, and to release some tension.

Coping with a crisis usually entailed a process of appraisal. This appraisal was not initially a conscious act. Rather, carers described a growing awareness of their own unhappiness, their own personal problems, the restrictions on their lives, their own needs and often feelings of guilt if they even dared to consider that they could not continue caring. While the crisis forced carers to confront the realities of their situation, appraisal was a period during which carers took 'a step back' and reviewed their situation. This was a potentially crucial point in carers' careers. This was the point at which carers could have decided that they were not going to continue caring and alternative arrangements would have been made. In carers' eyes, though, the only alternative would have been institutional care but this solution was totally unacceptable to them.

The appraisal process described by carers in the present study was similar to that contained within transactional models of stress and coping (Lazarus and Folkman, 1984; Lazarus, 1991; Pearlin, 1991). These models explain how when a potentially stressful demand or event occurs a primary appraisal takes place. This essentially involves an individual determining whether or not there is a need to respond to the event or demand. If there is not a perceived need to respond, then no action is taken. If there is a perceived need to respond, then a secondary appraisal is made. In this secondary appraisal an individual takes account of what resources they have available to meet the demand. A coping response, strategy or resource is then selected to deal with the event. If an individual feels that they can make an appropriate response this may lead to a new or fresh approach to coping. Following the appraisal process, some carers in the present study modified an existing routine or introduced a new one. Mrs Beaton, for example, introduced a new routine following her father's discharge from hospital, where he had been admitted because of her coping crisis. When coping is successful, a positive reappraisal of the self may also occur (Pearlin, 1991). This is similar to the experiences of some carers whose fresh approach and positive self-appraisal were described above. On the other hand, the model suggests that if individuals feel they cannot make an appropriate response a reappraisal may lead to stress being manifest in the expression of negative feelings. In the present study, carers who believed that they were unable to cope with caregiving were more likely to express negative feelings than those who felt they were coping. This highlights the fact that carers' responses to crises varied.

Carers' responses to crises

The function of crises was to force carers to consciously think about and confront the realities of their situation. For some carers, crises led to improved ways of coping. But this was not true of everyone. In accordance with this interpretation it is possible to describe three different responses to crises within the career of caregiving: the active, the passive and the expert.

Active response

Some carers whose caregiving career was characterised by increasing levels of stress and the development of carer expertise responded to crises in a proactive way. The crises that they experienced were positive in that they were the catalysts for constructive change. Following a period of appraisal as described above, carers subsequently adopted a more proactive approach to caregiving which included the setting of limits and being more assertive. Mrs Smith, for example, became more assertive and adopted a positive 'can-do' approach to her caring responsibilities and, most importantly of all, she accepted the situation. Carers who responded in this way can be likened to the 'balanced and boundary-setting' carers described by Twigg and Atkin (1994), in that following a crisis part of their positive reappraisal process was the adoption of a boundary-setting approach. In some cases this boundary setting extended to practical tasks too. Mrs Morrison, for example, steadfastly refused to take her mother-in-law out for a walk in her wheelchair. She claimed that her mother-in-law liked to draw attention to herself when she was out and that she found this behaviour embarrassing.

Passive response

Other carers whose caregiving career was characterised by increasing levels of stress, responded to crises in a more passive way. These carers differed from the active responders in two respects. Firstly, they appeared to develop little or no carer expertise. Secondly, their crises were not catalysts for positive change but rather were destructive in that they either caused carers to question their ability to cope, or they confirmed their belief that they could not. After a crisis these carers were unable to adopt a new approach, but rather continued to be overwhelmed by caregiving. These carers were more likely to resign themselves passively to the situation rather than accepting it and adopting a proactive approach. Some had tried unsuccessfully to seek help from service providers because they felt that they could no longer cope, but their failure to obtain help had lowered their self-esteem and confidence. Carers in this career were similar to the 'engulfed' carers in Twigg and Atkin's

(1994) typology in that caregiving had become the focus of their lives and they found it difficult to distance themselves from it. However, they differed from Twigg and Atkin's engulfed carers in one respect. Twigg and Atkin's engulfed carers tended to be wives or mothers of disabled children whereas in the current study carers in the passive career were more likely to be sons or daughters.

Expert response

The expert response stands outwith the other two. The caregiving career of these carers was marked by the absence of increasing levels of stress. This was the response of carers who said that they did not perceive caring as being stressful. They believed that they were coping well and were less likely to report having a crisis. These carers were more likely to already possess a degree of expertise than those in other careers. Many of them had been either trained or untrained nursing staff or had previously cared for other relatives. It seemed that previous experience, caregiving skills and confidence in their ability to cope with whatever came along protected them in some way from the stress that others experienced. This confidence and self-belief seemed to facilitate coping behaviours. These carers were similar to those described by Twigg and Atkins (1994) as being in the 'symbiotic' mode of caring, in that they gained in a positive way from their role and would not wish the responsibility to be taken from them. However, carers in the present study who demonstrated an expert response differed from Twigg and Atkin's carers in that they were more likely to be spouses rather than parents.

We can see from the responses outlined above that carers in the present study who had broadly similar careers responded in different ways to caregiving processes. The key issue in the processes described above is concerned with the nature of the appraisal process following a crisis. These were dynamic processes in that appraisal and coping influenced each other and were subject to change. When carers appraised a situation as potentially harmful, coping strategies were developed and pursued to reduce the perceived threat. Feedback from the coping process became part of a successive, almost subconscious, appraisal leading to modified coping, then further reappraisal and so on until a balance was reached. This process is what carers referred to as 'trial and error'. A crisis, though, by threatening to overwhelm carers' ability to cope, forced them to consciously reappraise their situation. A crisis could either be constructive or detrimental in that some carers subsequently modified their coping efforts by adopting a proactive approach, while others took a more passive stance.

How then do these experiences compare to those of other carers? In terms of the stresses faced and coping strategies used, the experiences of hidden carers are remarkably similar to those described by studies of carers visible to service providers (Kahana and Young, 1990; Murray and Livingston, 1998; Schofield et al., 1998; Braithwaite, 2000). The main difference lies in their perceptions of stress. The majority of carers in the present study found caring to be stressful but also that stress increased over time. This is contrary to a widely held understanding that carers suffer most stress at the start of their caregiving career (Kahana and Young, 1990; Brereton and Nolan, 2000) when they are relatively inexperienced but that stress reduces over time as carers gain experience in the tasks associated with caregiving. Carers who perceived themselves to be coping and who experienced positive outcomes from caregiving were the ones most likely to be gaining expertise and managing crises in a positive and proactive way. The development of expertise by hidden carers is similar to that described by other studies (Nolan et al., 2001; Llewellyn, 2003).

CHAPTER 5

From carer to client: pathways to providers

This chapter explores the stages of caring referred to as 'accessing services', 'carers as clients' and the 'continuation of caring'. It considers the reasons given by carers for not initially engaging with formal service providers, the pathways by which they made contact with providers, and the triggers to service receipt. The aim of the chapter is to explore how carers became clients and how they experienced the transition from hidden and unsupported to visible and supported caregiving. Support is defined as receiving assistance to sustain existing caregiving activities.

How many carers made this transition during the course of the study? At the start of the study, neither carers ($n = 26$) nor care recipients were receiving support from formal services. At stage two of the study, 9–12 months after initial contact was made, nine carers were receiving help from formal service providers, twelve continued to care without support and five had withdrawn from the study. Only two carers reported using private services. By stage three, conducted 24–28 months after the start of the study, the majority of carers had had some encounter with service providers. Only seven carers continued without support, and a further four had withdrawn. Ten were now using a wide range of services provided primarily by social services, which included day care, respite care, home care and the provision of aids and equipment. Of these, six also received a community nursing service. Two of the ten had comprehensive packages of care supplied by health and social care agencies, which included domiciliary care and community nursing. The two women who had used private services were no longer carers.

Reasons for non-use of services

In order to comprehend this transition from unsupported to supported caregiving, it is important to understand why carers had not originally been involved with formal services. Carers put forward a variety of reasons for their reluctance to become involved with formal service providers. They fell into four main groups, relating to the perceived authoritarian, and intrusive, nature of service providers; the wishes of care recipients; and difficulty in accessing services. Although each of these will be discussed individually, it is worth noting that carers frequently cited more than one reason for not using formal services.

The reason cited most often by carers was the perceived authoritarian nature of service providers. Some believed that to allow service providers into their homes led to a loss of control over their own lives and the caregiving situation. These perceptions were based on experience and anecdotal evidence. Individuals described how before they actually became a carer they had felt powerless during encounters with service providers, which took place either in their parent's house or in a hospital. These experiences made them determined not to accept help when they brought their relative to live with them:

> I don't trust official people. We like to keep to ourselves. Sometimes, a social worker would come in or even his nursing staff would come in and start telling me how to run his house. I said, 'now just wait a minute'. 'None of your bloody business' was my attitude to it. (Mr Brown, 40-year-old carer)

> I don't need or want [service providers'] help. There were times I don't want people coming in and telling me what to do. You feel that you were losing control ...You can't treat people like that. I just never think about accepting help. For all the wee problems I just get on with it. (Mrs Morrison, 58-year-old carer)

Services were also perceived as being intrusive. In order to accept the support offered by services, carers had to be prepared to trust strangers and let them intrude into their homes and lives. Some believed that it would be easier to accept help if they did not live in the same house as the care recipient. Then it would not be their lives, personal space or privacy that would be invaded. Preserving their privacy and control over events was important to carers:

> It is easier if you live in separate houses. It becomes easier to get someone in to help because *I* don't need a home help or a nurse. I feel they are intruding. I just feel that why should I have somebody into *my* house telling *me* what to do and going through *my* stuff when *I* don't need it. It's an intrusion, you feel the intrusion and it feels horrible. (Mrs Gordon, 63-year-old carer)

> I'm not awfully keen on social services. They think that can walk in a house and take over ... I'm kind of funny about having people coming in to my house. I like to be in charge and I like my own privacy too much. If I am unable to look after her, she will go in a home. (Mrs Beaton, 51-year-old carer)

Mrs Thompson had previously received regular visits from community nursing staff but cancelled them because she felt that she was no longer in control and that the acceptance of service support was increasingly restricting her life. She perceived that control of her life and the caregiving situation was back in her hands. She felt empowered and was determined to continue caring without practical support from formal services:

> Before I felt trapped and I felt I didn't have control of my own life any more. Someone else had taken control of it. Now I feel I have got control. And that feels good. Being a person who likes to control my own destiny, this having no control over anything was killing. I mean if I wanted to go out, I couldn't go out without having made sure the nurse had been first. (Mrs Thompson, 41-year-old carer)

These accounts raise the question of who is the focus of support: the carer or the care recipient. It also suggests that services provided to care recipients living in their own homes might be accepted more readily because they would not necessarily be seen as support for carers.

Often the wishes of the care recipient determined the acceptance of support. Refusals of help arose because care recipients shared the views of carers that formal service provision was intrusive. Carers responded to the care recipient's wishes by either never raising the subject of service receipt or not exploring the possibility of other types of support.

Carers said that to override the wishes of the care recipient caused more problems for them and they tended to take the path of least resistance. It appeared that to accept a service without the agreement of the care recipient could lead to tension and conflict within the caregiving relationship. Thus many carers preferred to continue without support if it meant that their relationship remained peaceful and harmonious.

> There's a limit to what I can do. I mean I can't turn round and say you've got to go [to the day centre], it would be nice, if she would go out for a couple of hours and give me some time to myself during the day but it doesn't work that way. So you just get on with it yourself. I don't want help to look after her because it makes more problems for me. Because then I've got to sit and listen to her moaning about people coming in and invading her privacy and wanting to know everything. (Mrs Veitch, 69-year-old carer)

> I always knew where the help was if I needed it — but my mother wouldn't accept it. It wasn't that I wouldn't accept it, it was my mother who wouldn't accept the help. My mother frowned on anybody coming through the door, definitely frowned upon it. Carers won't get help because it is the cared-for person who doesn't want help. It is better to be, it is easier — how can I put this — we have a helluva a time once that person goes, we have a worse time with the person. It is less hassle not having somebody here. Because if there is somebody here, well we used to have barneys [fights] about it. Aye, there is more of a hassle for us to ask for help if the person doesn't want it. It's more oh well, keep the peace. (Mrs Cranston, 50-year-old carer)

The above account illustrates how service receipt may be influenced by the preferences of the older person being cared for. With other client groups the carer is sometimes able to exert greater control. For example, the physical dependency and the lack of mental competence in someone with dementia allow carers and service providers to overlook their reluctance to accept services (Parker, 1993; Clarke, 1999). However, in the present study care recipients had no cognitive impairment and therefore had a degree of autonomy in making choices and enforcing them.

Only two carers in the study attributed their non-use of services to a lack of knowledge about 'the system' and availability of services. Both seemed to be completely unaware of what support was available or what help they might be entitled to. This made it more difficult for them to identify what help they required.

> I don't know what help there is in this area. But I'd probably ask at the health centre. They'd probably know and can supply the information if I needed it. Or maybe I would just go to the doctors I suppose. I don't know. No, I don't know anything really. I'm very naive. (Mrs Black, 47-year-old carer)

> Well you just don't know. You want help of some sort and you don't have any idea really of what's available or where to go. Nobody tells you what you are entitled to. Nobody tells you until you're a gibbering wreck. (Mrs Kearns, 37-year-old carer)

As we have seen, carers in the present study cited a number of reasons why they had no support from formal service providers. Despite their comments many carers did eventually accept help. We turn now to explore why and how this transition from hidden carer to service user took place.

How the transition was accomplished

How was this transition accomplished? There were four main pathways by which carers accessed service providers. Access to these pathways was via self-referral, GPs, hospital discharge procedures and carer support groups.

Self-referral

Self-referral was the least effective pathway to service providers. Although carers had expressed a reluctance to initiate contact with formal services some had tried and were left feeling very disappointed with their lack of progress and the time it took. In one example, while attempts at seeking help had resulted in a visit from a social worker, no services were forthcoming. Promises made were never kept and carers were left feeling bitter and disillusioned and that service providers had failed them at a time when they were most needed:

A nice person came from [social work] and I was thinking I was going to get help. I don't know exactly what's there. But I'm still waiting. (Mr Downs, 74-year-old carer)

I can't get two weeks' respite because of the incompetence of the social work department. There's too many people involved. You don't get a social worker now — you get care assessors and home care teams. I don't think I am asking for the earth, just a couple of weeks in the summer for respite and they are just totally ignoring my pleas. (Mr Brown, 40-year-old carer)

Carers believed that a self-referral was treated with less urgency than if a professional such as a GP or community nurse had made it. They perceived the referral and assessment procedure as a lengthy and drawn out process which created unnecessary delays. Delays, a seemingly inevitable feature of the journey to service receipt, increased carers' sense of helplessness and generated feelings of anger and frustration. Some carers, however, eventually succeeded in obtaining help directly from providers, though it took time:

I knew I needed to get help from somewhere. So I phoned everywhere and eventually I got put on to social work. He came out. I didn't really know though what they could do to help. I just knew I needed something but it took three months. (Mrs Veitch, 69-year-old carer)

I had been trying for three years. And one of the social workers said, 'but your referral only went in last November'. I said, 'I beg your pardon dear,' I said, 'my referral didn't go in one year ago, not two years ago but three years ago. You may not have put it forward but,' I said, 'it did go in and I have proof of that.' I said, 'I'll be back and I'll be back every week because my husband can't get out and in the bath.' So I went home and in about a fortnight the phone went. [The social worker said,] 'Would it be all right if I came on Thursday to see you?' 'Oh,' I said, 'by all means.' (Mrs Currie, 83-year-old carer)

General practitioners

The most common and most effective pathway to service providers was through general practitioners. GPs played a key role in helping carers to access services by referring them to other medical and social services. The role of GPs as gatekeepers to welfare services has long been recognised (Foster, 1983). Although helping carers is not a central aspect of their work, it was to GPs that the majority of carers in the present study said they would turn if they needed help and advice. Some reported that their GPs were very helpful and they felt well supported by them. They tended to praise their GPs for being sympathetic, for 'popping in' from time to time to see how they were, or for visiting them at regular intervals. In such instances carers felt that their GPs were aware of the difficulties they faced and regarded their needs as being just as important as those of the care recipient:

> If I want support then I'll get a hold of Dr Lance. He changed my life in that he made me see sense and that's why I go to him when I need that kind of support. (Mrs Thompson, 41-year-old carer)

> I was crying all the time. So the doctor put my dad in hospital for two weeks to give me a break because I was near breaking point and heading for a breakdown ... He's now in Mayfield [day centre] because she stepped in and done a report. My father was in there within two weeks when I was already told there was 40 people in front of him on the waiting list. (Mrs Watson, 38-year-old carer)

By contrast, other carers said that their GPs were unsupportive of their caring role. Such GPs were less likely to refer carers on to other services and left them with the feeling that there was nothing that could be done for them. In these cases carers felt that their GP either trivialised or overlooked their concerns:

> I was ready for a nervous breakdown. I went to see him and all he did was write this prescription for Prozac. That was his attitude, take a pill. (Mrs Kearns, 36-year-old carer)

This incident raises the question once again of who is the focus of service intervention. It also illustrates the way in which some GPs do not view family carers as a legitimate focus of their work (PRTC, 1999). The patient or care recipient whose health is compromised is their priority. It was sometimes only when the carer's health broke down that unsupportive GPs took cognisance of their caregiver role. In Mrs Tierney's case, it was only when she collapsed at home and required an emergency admission to hospital that her GP acknowledged her caregiving responsibilities. Since his carer was unable to look after him, Mrs Tierney's husband was admitted to hospital until she had recovered. They were both discharged on the same day with the promise of support services.

> I feel very bitter about it. When you come out of hospital, when you're looking after somebody and you are feeling terrible, you're really ill. I mean as you get older it takes you longer and longer to get over major surgery. Yet I'm still expected to look after him, I'm still responsible. I got a phone call saying that Mrs M. would be up to see me the next day. I thought Mrs M was a home help. Mrs M. never came. About five weeks after I was out of hospital Mrs M. came up and she was head of the home helps. (Mrs Tierney, 68-year-old carer)

In this instance, it was unclear who was the main focus of service support, Mrs Tierney or her husband. Both needed help and could therefore be regarded as care recipients. Mrs Tierney, however, believed that services were being provided to enable her, the carer, to continue caregiving. While this is exactly what many carers would like, Mrs Tierney did not: she wanted someone else to take responsibility for her husband's care.

Planned discharge from hospital

The second most common pathway to service providers was through the discharge of the care recipient from hospital following a planned or emergency admission. Carers were unsure who within the hospital staff was responsible for their referral to social services but assumed that it was the hospital consultant. Through this pathway, two carers had a comprehensive package of health and social care arranged as part of the discharge planning procedure, and others accessed aids, equipment, home and day care. In these situations carers seemed to be reluctant or incapable of opposing the wishes of the hospital staff who made the referral for assessment. They preferred instead to adopt a 'wait and see' approach. If the services offered were perceived by carers as being beneficial, then they remained in place. If they proved troublesome or too intrusive carers were quick to cancel them.

Some carers reported that support services were arranged without their knowledge. It was only through phone calls or visits from service providers once the care recipient was home from hospital that carers became aware that they had been referred. This seemed to happen because of the way hospital procedures were followed. Carers were often absent when the care recipient's treatment was being considered by clinical staff. As a consequence sometimes decisions were made without consultation with carers, or they were left in ignorance of important facts that could affect their situation. For example, some carers were told that an assessment of their relative's needs had been carried out but that no support had been arranged because the care recipient had insisted that no help was required.

> The hospital said that they had done an assessment of her needs before she came out. But unfortunately, the social worker spoke to my mum and asked, 'do you need a home help, do you need this, that or the other?' And she said, 'Oh I don't need it, my daughter does all that for me.' And that was that ... So they did a re-assessment after she was home. She came home about the beginning of September and the home help started in October. (Mrs Kearns, 37-year-old carer)

This case illustrates how service providers often overlook the needs of carers and how caregivers are unaware of their right to a community care assessment. It also highlights the potential conflict of interests between the needs of care recipients and carers.

Carer support groups

The fourth pathway to providers was through carer support groups. Support groups played a crucial role in helping carers to access services. As one of the few forms of support directly provided for carers, they are important sources of information about benefits, support and advocacy services. As many carers lacked the knowledge and the confidence to make contact with service providers directly, carers groups did so on their behalf. Moreover, the importance of their work in supporting carers seemed to be acknowledged, and any referral they made to service providers was acted upon quickly:

> The Carers Association contacted them. I have had Mandy who runs it out, she came in to see my mum. I must admit after that [social work] weren't long in coming out. (Mrs Davidson, 68-year-old carer)

Carers' support groups were valued highly by those who made use of them. They also played a key role in enabling people to see themselves as carers, and as such this identity sometimes became important in making them more assertive in seeking help. Moreover, hearing about the success of others in the support group was encouraging, and once carers had an initial encounter with service providers that resulted in a positive outcome they were much more willing to instigate further contact:

> I'm not frightened now to ask. Knowing [what is available] makes a difference. I know some of the stuff [services] is no use at all but there might be things that you think, hey that might make a difference. (Mrs Kearns, 37-year-old carer)

> I phone up and asked if I could apply again. I was told go ahead and apply. Kay [social worker] said I might get a community care grant because of my dad being in hospital. I'm going to apply for trousers and things. (Mrs Watson, 38-year-old carer)

From having no contact at all at stage one of the present study, by stage three some carers were keen to get whatever help they could. But why and under what circumstances did they change their minds about service support?

Reasons for the transition

In most instances, the transition to supported caring was as a result of crises in caregiving, where carers expressed feelings of being unable to cope any longer and there was a sense of urgency about the whole experience.

> It was a pretty bad time and I just felt the world was caving in. I felt that I'd got older and I couldn't cope suddenly, you feel as if you

can't sleep, your mind's in a turmoil. I thought I was going to end up a nervous wreck on tablets and taken away to a psychiatrist's or something. I had just reached a peak and knew I had to get help. (Mrs Peters, 47-year-old carer)

In other cases, critical incidents rather than crises were the catalyst which led to accepting or seeking support from formal services. Critical incidents differed in nature to coping crises in that carers did not experience the same sense of urgency. Neither did they make carers feel as though they could no longer cope. Rather, these incidents added to the demands made on them, and the decision to engage with service providers was not sudden but reached in a more gradual manner. Incidents of this nature included periods of ill health of the carer or other family member such as sons and daughters or close friends.

[The GP] arranged the assessment and I got respite ... It just felt at times as though it was never ending for us. Things had to change because at the time my husband was flat out on his back. It was just far too much. So that's when I started putting her in [respite] and I tried to keep it going because it was working and I don't see why I should change it and go back to the way things were. (Mrs Duncan, 47-year-old carer)

Experience of services

How did the realities of service receipt compare to carers' perceptions? Did it overcome previous doubts or were their fears confirmed? On the whole, for carers who ultimately perceived their need for support as overwhelming, the actual experience of service receipt did not match their preconceived ideas. Although services such as home care and community nursing were not widely used, they were valued by those who did receive them. The intrusive nature of the service became less important once its value was established.

It is just amazing the difference it makes. You know just with that bit of help in the morning, it just makes things so much easier. Just having that space, the rest of it has fallen into place. (Mrs Kearns, 37-year-old carer)

Carers who perceived services to be authoritarian and intrusive in nature resolved their concern by accepting more readily the least invasive services. A request for the aids and equipment service was often carers' first contact with providers. These services were not regarded as being intrusive, nor did they entail letting strangers into their homes on a regular or routine basis. Indeed, once the equipment had been obtained there was no need to maintain contact with providers.

Because service provision took place outwith the home and only for a pre-determined period of time, these services were less intrusive in nature and no invasion of carers' space occurred. When arranging respite or day care the care recipient's compliance was important and was gained by reframing the meaning of the service. For example, some carers found respite care more acceptable if it was thought of as a 'holiday' to which the care recipient was entitled. This seemed to give their requests for respite a legitimacy that did not generate feelings of guilt.

Criticisms of services

Criticism was levelled at difficulties in accessing services. Access was constrained by complex administrative procedures and poor communication. Service receipt is the product of negotiation with service providers (Twigg and Atkin, 1994; Wuest, 2000). Yet, rather than seeing it as a process of negotiation, carers in the present study tended to talk in terms of it being a 'fight' and that they had to battle for what they wanted.

> It's all the fighting you have to do. I don't mean fighting exactly, but it's all this telephoning you have to do. You're on the phone, you're down at the office and yet nothing gets done. I mean, what's the point of it, all that red tape, that's what it is. That is what makes you so angry. I didn't ask for a lot but I didn't get anything so I'm not going to ask for help. What's the point? I am an old age pensioner looking after a pensioner who could trip over anything and then what would they do. It would cost them thousands to look after my mother if I wasn't able. (Mrs Bennet, 67-year-old carer)

Access to day care seemed to be even more restricted than respite because carers were generally unable to make referrals themselves. Access was usually via a referral from a GP, social worker or hospital consultant. While in theory this service might be supplied for the benefit of the care recipient, in the present study it was usually arranged to benefit carers who regarded it as short-term respite. Once obtained, those who used it valued it highly because it was normally provided on a regular basis, with some care recipients attending on two, three or four days a week. Its function was supportive rather than therapeutic.

Unfamiliarity with procedures, along with a feeling of being let down by 'the system', caused a great deal of stress and anger among carers. Carers did not seem to understand the processes and patterns of social work practice. For example, some carers who had received respite care on more than one occasion found that each request was followed by an assessment. They felt that this was unnecessary since the cared-for person's condition remained unchanged.

Carers expected social workers to operate in a way similar to GPs in that they were assigned to a particular one whom they could contact when required. They failed to understand the case closure system that required a re-referral each time assistance was needed. This system was confusing to carers who expected to be able to contact the social worker they last dealt with. Carers' confusion about the system underpinned their comments about phoning up only to be told, 'Oh she's left, I'll get someone to contact you,' and they found themselves still waiting. Thus, carers experienced the system of referral and assessment for services as inefficient, unreliable and frustrating, and some had taken to making their own arrangements.

Experience taught carers that they had to be assertive and determined in order to access services. To them the referral and assessment procedure seemed a lengthy and drawn out process which created unnecessary delays. Delays, a seemingly inevitable feature of the journey to service receipt, increased their sense of helplessness and generated feelings of anger and frustration.

Interactions that had no positive outcomes for carers were viewed as a disappointing experience and, for less determined individuals, one they were keen not to repeat. It also confirmed carers' perceptions that formal service providers were unreliable and inefficient. Thus unproductive interactions sometimes led to withdrawal of contact and a renewed determination not to seek service support again. They felt that they did not need help badly enough to want to fight what they saw as the bureaucracy of the system:

> I phoned to see what help I could get. I thought because of my age and my arthritis we would surely get something. Then I got a letter back saying somebody was coming and they never turned up. But then eventually a man did come one day and sat there and talked but nothing ever happened. You see, I didn't know about anything. I've never had anything to do with anybody like that in my life. (Mrs Yuill, 75-year-old carer)

Unassertive carers were easily deterred from pursuing the matter and, having experienced difficulties in bringing their situation to the attention of service providers, they simply gave up trying. By the time her caregiving role ended with her husband's death, Mrs Yuill had received no support whatsoever from formal service providers despite her own frailty.

Once embarked upon the journey to service receipt, carers' experiences of services varied and their pattern of use was irregular. Davidson and Reed (1995) have likened the experiences of people embarking on a career as a client of services to stepping onto a moving escalator. It can be difficult to get on this escalator but, once on board, the user is carried on towards increased dependency. The opposite process is refusing to accept or cancelling services, thus moving to less dependency. Once older people are on the escalator, they are more likely to be offered other types of care that minimise risk but increase their dependency further (Davidson and Reed, 1995).

The experiences of hidden carers, however, contradict Davidson and Reed's views. In the current study it was younger rather than older people who once in receipt of services seemed reluctant to step off the moving escalator. In some cases, they remained on the care escalator in order to pre-empt future problems because they anticipated difficulty in regaining services if required in the future. In contrast, older service users stepped on and off as it suited them. They were more likely to try out a service and then cancel if it proved unsuitable. A possible explanation for these differences might be that caregiving created more conflicting demands on younger carers then on older ones whose children had grown up. They perhaps remained on the care escalator because the receipt of formal services benefited not just the care recipient but the whole family unit. For younger carers whose caregiving role caused marital problems, increasing service use often reduced the tension within their personal relationships. Older service users did not experience the same conflicting demands on their time between caring and the needs of a young family. To them, service use was more intrusive and therefore less welcome.

Power dynamics

The inherently unequal relationship between carers and providers was the main factor determining carers' non-use of services. As previously stated, becoming a client of services is a process of negotiation (Twigg and Atkin, 1994, Wuest, 2000). It also involves negotiating a power relationship. Although few carers spoke directly about this power dynamic, they alluded to it often and their awareness of it underpinned their behaviour and perceptions.

Carers' accounts illustrate the power dynamics that exist between service users and providers. In this chapter we have seen how carers experienced access to services as conflict, how they perceived professionals as authoritarian and how some felt unable to exercise their power. We also saw how the needs of carers tended to be overlooked when care recipients were being discharged from hospital. These are all examples of interactions between carers and service providers where the balance of power was inherently unequal.

Seeking or receiving help requires that carers offer themselves up as a client. Service providers establish and maintain control over clients through ownership of knowledge and resources (Clarke, 1999). By exercising the authority vested in them by law, providers control clients' access to and receipt of services. Service receipt hinges on assessment; a process that evaluates carers' lives and determines their eligibility for services (McDonald, 1999). The assessment process can be likened to the ritualistic admission practices in the institutions studied by Foucault (1979), whereby prisoners or inmates of asylums are stripped of their identity in order to reclassify them as objects. This is a process that objectifies, silences, dominates and exposes people to public scrutiny (Foucault, 1979).

In an assessment for services, carers and care recipients are similarly stripped of their identity and their right to privacy, and are expected to divulge personal and intimate details of their lives, while the professional keeps theirs private. The assessment objectifies carers as clients and exposes them to the public gaze. Having their lives examined in this way, in the face of someone who is not in a similarly exposed position, creates a powerful dynamic in which the carer or client is vulnerable and dominated and forced to rely on the goodwill and knowledge of the professional in allocating services. This dynamic places the carer or client in a dependent and less powerful position. In becoming a client, carers change identity and become an object for scrutiny and surveillance by professionals.

It was the fear of service providers' authority and control over their lives that often discouraged carers from seeking their support. They initially resisted the power of service providers by refusing to engage with them, but eventually the demands of caregiving were such that they needed support to continue. Nonetheless, carers resisted service providers' control and authority in a variety of ways. Firstly, since control is related to decision-making (Lukes, 1987) carers resisted service providers' power by challenging their decisions. This usually took the form of refusing offers of services or equipment that providers had decided would be beneficial. Mrs Duncan, for example, despite admitting her need for help, refused the offer of day care for her mother. Mrs Watson would not allow her father to be admitted to long-term care, nor would she accept a standing frame for her father that the physiotherapist thought would be helpful.

Secondly, carers exercised power and maintained control by placing limits on the type of help they would accept. The majority accepted only the least intrusive forms of support, such as respite and day care services, that were provided outwith the carer or care recipient's home. The conflict that carers experienced in their interactions with service providers illustrated their attempts to redress the balance of power. Conflict was generated by both parties trying to pursue their own interests. Carers generally had an idea of what type of support they wanted and when. Professionals, on the other hand, were trying to assess and meet carers' needs within the restrictions of local budgets and service availability.

Fundamental differences in the relationship between service providers and carers have been highlighted by Allen (2000), who claims that they are based on who is seen as having the 'prized' knowledge and where expertise is seen to lie. Hidden carers have learnt their skills by trial and error and often have a better understanding of the caregiving situation than service providers. This 'expertise' should not threaten the relationship between carers and service providers. All knowledge should be seen as being equally important and acknowledgement of this should lead to a partnership approach between carers and services providers.

CHAPTER 6

Carers: partners in the provision of care?

This book began by setting the experiences of carers in the context of current policy, which seeks to promote carers as key partners in the provision of care (Scottish Executive 2001b, 2006b). Being partners in the provision of care implies that carers and service providers must work together to achieve common goals. Their relationship should be based on mutual respect for each other's skills and competencies. It should also recognise the advantages of combining their resources to achieve positive outcomes for the carer and cared-for person.

A partnership in care can only exist if either the carer or the cared-for person is in receipt of support services. Yet one of the remaining unresolved issues of caregiving is the paradoxical situation where, despite increasing attention and resources being focused on developing support services, relatively few carers actually use them. The other unresolved issue is determining when and in what way it is most appropriate to offer help and support to carers (Aneshensel et al., 1995).

Temporal approaches such as the one adopted in this book have helped to shed light on the experiences of carers and the issue of the timing of service interventions. The temporal model of care emerging from carers' experiences indicates that 'hidden' caregiving is only one of a number of stages that caregivers go through and that there are specific times in their career when carers are more receptive to service intervention. The model suggests that during the early stages of their career, carers are least likely to accept service intervention. It is only during the later stages of caregiving that carers are more likely to seek and accept support. The nine stages in this temporal model and their implications for policy and practice are outlined below.

Temporal model of caring

Dawning realisation

Caregiving begins with this embryonic phase called 'dawning realisation'. Without exception, carers can recall the events which led to them becoming a carer. This stage is characterised by carers' realisation that their relative is unable to do things for themselves and needs more help than usual. This realisation can happen either suddenly or gradually depending on the nature of events leading up to the 'dawning realisation'. In situations where a sudden injury or illness is the catalyst for becoming a carer, the realisation is swift. On the other hand, where the older person experiences a gradual deterioration in their health, realisation tends to be slow and gradual. The pace of this stage is not necessarily determined by residency, although many carers who shared a household with the person being cared for reported a gradual awareness of how they were increasingly doing more for their relative.

During this stage carers also realised that their relationship with the person needing care was undergoing a fundamental change, which entailed a reversal of roles. No longer were they, for example, parent and adult child, rather they were becoming adult child carer and cared-for parent. Similarly, the relationship between spouses became one of carer and cared-for rather than a more equal partnership. Carers confronted questions relating to their ability and duty: rhetorical questions such as 'why me?', 'can I do it?', 'should I do it?', and 'if I don't — then what are the consequences?' These questions were not usually fully articulated or discussed with service providers or other family members. Nor were they answered, if at all, until the following stage.

Adopting the carer role

This second stage was characterised by carers' acceptance of their relative's need for care and of their responsibility for providing it. This acceptance was often based on the belief that no one else was available or able to provide the care required. Carers subconsciously considered alternatives such as care homes, deemed them unsuitable and accepted that they should become the main carer. During this process carers answered the rhetorical questions posed by themselves at the previous stage, i.e. 'can I do it?', 'should I do it?', and 'if I don't — then what are the consequences?' Only in very few cases were these questions discussed openly before the role was finally accepted.

In accepting the caregiving role, people tended to build on past relationships. Where caring represented the continuation of an established relationship, these questions were rarely raised and there was no decision to make. For example, in the case of a spouse there was often little hesitation, but rather a strong desire to accept the caring role. In other cases, carers who had poor relationships with the person requiring care accepted the role with great reluctance. They were motivated by a sense of obligation and duty rather than affection.

'Dawning realisation' and 'adopting the carer role' were important stages in the caregiving career. The most crucial aspect of this stage for them was the decision-making process. Yet carers sometimes felt that they had not been offered the opportunity to make a fully informed decision or indeed a choice. Many of them said that they 'had no choice' but to provide care. When carers had the choice of taking on the caring role, they perceived themselves as having had control over their decision. Where there appeared to be an absence of choice, often no clear positive decision was made by the carer.

For many carers, their first interaction with service providers often occurred during these first two stages, particularly if their relative had been hospitalised. Carers' criticism of providers at this stage centred on their lack of concern about carers' ability to undertake the required level of care, a lack of consultation and the assumption by clinical staff that individuals were willing and able to become the main carer for their relative.

This lack of consultation, and these assumptions, by clinical staff about carers' ability and willingness to care is concerning, especially since the Carers Strategy was intended to mark a 'decisive change' in policy and practice. It included proposals that should enable carers to choose to care or not, to be adequately prepared to care, to receive relevant help at an appropriate stage, and to be enabled to care without it adversely affecting their health or inclusion in society. The strategy placed particular emphasis on providing support at key transition points, particularly at the beginning and end of care.

Most fundamental of all was the notion of choice, with the intention of policy, as stated in the Carers Strategy, to 'support people who choose to be carers' (Scottish Executive, 1999). This suggests that policy recognises that the transition into caregiving is a crucial phase and that when this occurs suddenly there is a need to exercise an informed choice about whether or not to become a carer. However, the findings from the present study suggest that, in reality, exercising such choice and having control over the situation is extremely difficult for many carers. The majority of them felt that they had no choice and little control over whether or not to become a carer. Furthermore, the Community Care and Health (Scotland) Act (2002) placed a statutory responsibility on the NHS to identify carers, inform them of their rights and refer them to other agencies where appropriate. The most appropriate time for this to take place is when the person requiring care is in hospital or during the discharge planning process. Yet, according to the experiences carers reported here, it would seem that a carer awareness approach has not yet been incorporated into the practice of clinical staff and health care agencies.

Going it alone

'Going it alone' represented the period after individuals had accepted their role and identified themselves as a carer. This, the third stage in the caregiving career, was the period in which carers looked after their relative without support from formal service providers. In terms of length it could vary from months to several years. Some carers had some limited support from their social networks, but it tended to be short-lived. Carers reported that family and friends soon left them to 'get on with it' and expressed regret at the loss of friendships.

This was the phase in which the concept of control was most apparent. Carers who brought a care recipient to live with them tended to feel in control of the caregiving situation. This was in contrast to carers who moved into the home of the care recipient and who felt that they had little control or say in what took place. However, in cases where the care recipient was too frail or ill to exercise power, carers were able to maintain control. This desire for control also impacted upon their decisions about using services. Some carers had been offered a referral to health and social care agencies but refused the opportunity because of their perceptions of service providers as being authoritarian and intrusive. Thus, for the majority, their caregiving activities went completely unacknowledged by formal service providers.

Concern over service users' and carers' perceptions of service providers is not new (Sinclair, 1994). Moreover, a desire for control and negative perceptions of service providers among users and carers has been acknowledged in recent policy documents (Scottish Executive, 2006a, 2006c). Following a major review of the way in which social services are delivered in Scotland, the report *Changing Lives* makes a number of recommendations that seek to change the way in which social service workers are perceived. The report acknowledges that the therapeutic relationship between social workers and individuals such as carers is critical for achieving successful outcomes. It identifies common elements in successful interventions as empathy; warmth and respect; a mutual understanding and agreement; and a person-centred approach (Scottish Executive, 2006c: 28). A person-centred approach is taken to mean using the perspective and concepts of the client or, in some cases, carers. If importance is being placed on the centrality of this relationship, then there is hope that in the future service providers will be regarded with less suspicion and fewer carers will be inhibited from accepting service interventions because of negative perceptions.

Gaining expertise

This stage was characterised by carers' ability to learn from their experience and eventually to be able to carry out routine procedures that were once unfamiliar, in a competent and proficient manner. When they became carers, the majority of individuals had limited caregiving skills. Most took on the role without fully appreciating the nature or extent of the care they were expected to provide. Many were ill-prepared for their role, and were given no training and little information or advice even when caregiving followed a planned discharge from hospital. Those who had previous experience, either of caring or of having worked as a nurse, were more likely to adapt quickly to the practical aspects of the role. Others had to rely on their own initiative.

Carers gained experience and developed skills in caregiving through a process of trial and error. When faced with a problem they would consider the range of resources available and decide on a particular action. If that strategy was effective, then it was used again if and when required. If it was found to be ineffective, consideration was again given to the problem and another possible solution identified. This process continued until effective strategies were identified and used routinely. Thus, through a continuous process of trial and error, carers progressed from being relative novices to being competent and proficient in the activities and management of caregiving.

Expertise was acquired through practical experience and entailed an intuitive grasp of a situation based on an understanding of its important aspects. Thus carers developed expertise through experience and their intimate knowledge of the situation. This expertise allowed them to notice and attend to any changes in the care recipient's condition quickly. However, carers developed expertise in varying degrees. Those who gained a great deal of expertise and who felt competent were more likely to cope with caregiving. Many regarded themselves as experts in the care of their relative.

The acknowledgment that carers are experts in the care of their relative is important for the therapeutic relationship between caregivers and service providers. Carers in the study reported here, however, claimed that service providers failed to acknowledge their expertise and tried to tell them what to do and how to do it. This failure to recognise carers' expertise was one of the factors that alienated carers and caused them to withdraw from further interaction with service providers. The key to successful partnerships is for service providers to recognise that carers are experts too.

This process of gaining expertise should be promoted and encouraged by service providers. Although a small amount of training for carers is already available, it is not available widely, and particularly not to carers who are unknown to service providers. In their response to *The Future of Unpaid Care in Scotland*, the Scottish Executive has made training for carers a priority. Training is to be provided by Carers Scotland and funded directly by the Executive. It is to be hoped that training will help build carers' capacity to undertake the practical tasks involved in caregiving and also encourage service providers to acknowledge this expertise. Training may also support carers to continue providing care for a longer period than might otherwise be possible.

Sinking or swimming

The term 'sinking or swimming' is derived from carers' references to coping. Sinking referred to feeling overwhelmed and unable to cope, while swimming implied coping by being on top of things. Carers described how they seemed to move in and out of phases of 'sinking' or 'swimming'. Mrs Thompson, for example, explained that:

> It gets more stressful ... It is all the wee things that get you down and because they are getting older and keep expecting more of you. [Caring] either makes you sink or swim. Well, I did sink but then I swam and then I sunk again but now ... well I am still standing here. I've come through it. (Mrs Thompson, 43-year-old carer)

As caregiving progressed it became more stressful, even though carers become more competent and experienced. Stress had a cumulative effect in that one stressor like incontinence or demanding behaviour by the cared-for person would beget another, such as tiredness in the carer. Behaviours such as these have been described in Gilhooley's (1987) study of carers of people with dementia as 'acts of omission' and 'acts of commission'. Included in 'acts of omission' was a lack of concern with personal hygiene, apathy and disinterest in conversation. 'Acts of commission' included such behaviours as attention seeking and incontinence. Of these categories of behaviours, Gilhooley found that 'acts of omission' were much less stressful for carers than 'acts of commission'. Although carers clearly develop a range of coping strategies, such as the use of routines to deal with such challenges, they took different approaches to problem-solving.

When faced with crises or critical incidents, carers either sank or swam. Swimming was associated with an active response to crises, the presence of positive outcomes from which carers derived satisfaction, and caregiver control. Strategies such as seeking information and planning in advance were indicative of an active approach. In contrast, sinking was associated with a passive response, the presence of negative outcomes which caused carers to feel depressed and overwhelmed by caregiving, and a lack of control. Examples of passive responses included using music or alcohol to escape from the stress of caring.

Feelings of being in control had important implications for carers' perceptions of coping and for their interactions with service providers. Carers who felt in control of caregiving tended to perceive themselves as coping. If they felt they were coping, carers were less likely to want or seek support from service providers. High levels of expertise in terms of having the necessary skills, knowledge and emotional support were also associated with an increasing ability to cope. The more competent and in control carers felt the less likely they were to be overwhelmed by the demands of caregiving. On the other hand, carers who were not in control of caregiving perceived themselves as not coping.

Moving on from this stage to the next depended on the extent to which carers felt that they were coping or not. If they felt that they were coping and in control, then they were more likely to continue for longer without service intervention. On the other hand, those who felt overwhelmed and unable to cope were more likely to seek or accept support from service providers. Crises in coping were the most common catalyst for seeking help and so help-seeking was associated with a sense of failure and a loss of control.

These findings suggest that carers should be encouraged and supported to develop coping strategies that are most appropriate for their particular style of coping and caring situation. This could easily be incorporated into the planned training for carers mentioned above. Future crises may be averted if proposed policy is embedded in practice. Policy for carers adopts a preventative approach which aims to identify them as early as possible in their caregiving career and refer them to appropriate sources of support as soon as possible in order to prevent crises and ill health (Scottish Executive, 2006b). Furthermore, a focus on carers' health is to be included in other health improvement initiatives and in a Review of Nursing in the Community currently being undertaken. If, however, policy aims to support carers and avoid crises and the breakdown of the caregiving situation, this measure cannot be taken in isolation. Future crises in coping may also be avoided if service providers' response to self-referrals from carers is prompt and effective.

Putting plans into place to support carers by training and a preventative approach are all very positive steps. Service providers, however, must also recognise that, contrary to current belief, the most stressful time for carers is not necessarily at the start of caring when they are relatively inexperienced. Carers have reported that despite gaining expertise caring actually becomes more stressful as time goes on. This is a point that service providers must take on board. Service providers cannot assume that experience leads to reduced levels of stress.

Accessing services

This stage was characterised by attempts to access services. These attempts were usually triggered by crises, which encouraged carers to seek and accept help, although the process was not straightforward. A number of pathways were used to access services, the most effective of which was via GPs. The least effective was self-referral. Those who tried but failed to seek help directly from providers were left feeling bitter, disempowered and disillusioned with the system.

These findings suggest that service providers need to be aware that carers making a self-referral are often in a crisis situation and should be given priority. Making the referral system more effective for carers may require a change in practice. Current practice, according to the testimony of carers, is that referrals from GPs and carer support groups are acted upon more quickly than self-referrals. This is a very disempowering practice which causes carers to lose faith and become disillusioned with the welfare system. The process of self-referral needs to be simplified and made more straightforward. When dealing with referrals, service providers also need to be sensitive to carers' feelings of failure. This is an area which policy does not address. Proposed changes to social work practice described in the *Changing Lives* report may address this issue. *Changing Lives* (Scottish Executive, 2006c) aims to improve the way in which services are organised and delivered. The report makes a commitment to carers and service users that service providers will focus on the things that make a difference to people's lives. Improving the speed at which self-referrals are acted upon would certainly make a difference to carers' lives.

Carers experienced access to services as a lengthy, protracted process fraught with difficulties, which they referred to as 'a fight' or 'a battle'. Since carers did not perceive themselves as being the focus of service intervention, they resented having to ask for help. Having to engage in a 'battle' to get help fuelled their antagonism towards what they referred to as 'failures of the system'. Attempts to get help highlighted the power of service providers, who controlled carers' access to services by exercising the authority vested in them by law. This confirmed carers' perceptions of them as being authoritarian in nature. Carers were aware of the power of service providers and alluded to it indirectly when talking about how service intervention might lead to a potential loss of independence and control. Although service intervention helped carers to cope, some still had difficulty in doing so. Also, service intervention could create problems as well as resolving them, and so the cycle of sinking or swimming continued.

Sometimes the decision to accept service intervention was taken out of the carer's hands. If the care recipient was admitted to hospital, services were sometimes arranged as part of a planned discharge procedure. In these cases, referral was sometimes made without consultation with carers. Yet this stage provided the ideal opportunity for service providers to view carers as 'partners in care' and in this way support their efforts to cope and continue caring. This stage also illustrates the importance of the policy for the NHS to implement carers information strategies. Under the Community Care and Health (Scotland) Act 2002, NHS Boards and their employees are required to inform carers of their rights. This measure should make an appreciable difference to the lives of carers in the sorts of situations described above. It should also ensure that carers are consulted and their views taken into consideration whenever any decisions are being made about the person being cared for.

Carers as clients

This stage was characterised by carers' acceptance of service intervention in order to prevent the breakdown of care. This stage was closely linked to the previous one and refers to the status of carers, which changed to that of a client once contact was made with service providers. 'Carers as clients' is one of the ways in which carers are conceptualised by service providers (Twigg, 1989).

Although many carers would like to have continued without service support, for many there came a point when they realised it was not in their best interests to continue without help. Acceptance of formal services was often associated with feelings of failure and relinquishing control of the caregiving situation. It was also in some cases determined by the wishes of the care recipient and took place only with their co-operation.

Carers did not however, unquestioningly accept service providers' recommendations for particular services. The least intrusive services, such as day or respite care and aids and equipment, were the ones most acceptable to carers. While home care services were not widely used, carers who accepted them usually appreciated them once they recognised the benefits.

Although they finally accepted services, carers were emphatic that it is not they that needed help but rather the person they were looking after. They did not view themselves as clients and were aware that formal services are traditionally designed to meet the needs of care recipients. This was one reason why carers were reluctant to admit service providers into their homes. They did not want strangers coming into *their* home and intruding on *their* privacy when it is not they who were the clients in need of help. Nonetheless, a service such as respite care was frequently arranged because carers were regarded as clients in need of a break.

Continuation of caring

Service intervention marked a new stage in carers' careers. Caregiving continued but now with support from service providers. Carers had successfully negotiated the pathway to providers and for some there was a steady increase in the level of support they received. Thus carers had increasing levels of interaction with providers, such as paid care workers who came into their homes or staff in day or respite care facilities. This stage was also marked by the adoption of new routines which were developed to take account of service intervention. For example, ensuring that the care recipient was up and dressed in readiness for day care required a change to existing routines. Similarly, ensuring that clean equipment and laundry was available should community nurses need it required a change to household routines.

Service receipt also created tension. Carers reported that interactions with service providers could be frustrating and stressful. Criticisms of service providers were based on their apparent disregard for carers' specialist knowledge and expertise about the needs of the care recipient. Carers felt that while they might have been regarded by service providers as clients, they were certainly not seen as 'experts' or 'partners'.

An issue highlighted by the last three stages — 'accessing services', 'carers as clients' and 'continuation of caring' — and addressed by recent legislation is the question of who should be the focus of service intervention: the carer or the care recipient? Services have traditionally been designed to meet the needs of carers rather than the cared-for person, so professionals tend to view carers as clients. Yet, as we have seen, some carers do not see themselves as being in need of help. According to them it is the cared-for person who needs help and who should therefore be the focus of intervention. Moreover, carers suggested that they would be more likely to accept services if they were not the ones being identified as being 'needy'. This is exactly the point made by the Scottish Carers Legislation Working Group (2001), which argued that carers were in a unique position in that they only required support because of their relationship to another person whose care they were responsible for.

The level and type of support required by carers is determined by an assessment of their needs. According to the temporal model of care, 'accessing services' would be the most appropriate stage for carers to have an assessment. Yet carers did not seem to be aware of having had an assessment, nor were they aware of their right to one. They were, however, aware that the care recipient had undergone an assessment, and spoke about this often in some detail. Yet in order to receive services carers must have had an assessment without necessarily realising what was taking place. If carers were unaware of being assessed, this calls into question the approach taken by the service provider who conducted the assessment, who perhaps did not make it sufficiently clear what the purpose of the assessment was and who was being assessed. This suggests that there is room for improvement in the way in which carers' assessments are conducted.

The issue about who is the focus of intervention has been addressed by the Community Care and Health (Scotland) Act 2002, which introduced new rights for carers. By placing a duty on local authorities to take account of carers' views when undertaking an assessment of a cared-for person, this legislation recognises carers as key partners in the provision of care. The key to the successful implementation of the measures introduced by this legislation is the process of assessment. Under this legislation carers are entitled to an assessment of their own needs regardless of whether the care recipient is also undergoing an assessment. Although carers have been entitled to an assessment of their needs for the past decade, the main change brought about by this legislation is that the needs of carers are to be seen as part of the overall package of care for the person being cared for. In this context the purpose of assessment should now be to determine how the care needs of the cared-for person are to be met and how responsibility for their care will be shared between the carers and other service providers.

This is an important measure because it clarifies the issue of who formal services are for. By providing services to support carers as part of the package designed to meet the needs of the care recipient, the Community Care and Health (Scotland) Act 2002 should encourage carers to accept support. Moreover, by viewing carers as partners this legislation marks an important change in the way carers are to be treated in both individual caring situations and planning systems. This should ultimately change the balance of power between carers and service providers. This has important implications because carers in the present study were aware of service providers exercising their power and authority over them and determining their access to services. This was one reason why some carers were averse to seeking or accepting support from them. By changing the status of carers from client to partner, this legislation should empower carers and enable them to engage more readily with service providers.

New horizons

'New horizons' refers to the stage when, for what ever reasons, carers were no longer required to provide care. The end of caregiving was due to the death of the care recipient; an alternative caregiver taking over; admission to long-term care; or the failing health or illness of the carer. At this final stage in their caregiving trajectory, carers experienced a mixture of emotions. Some experienced feelings of sadness tinged with relief that caregiving had finally come to an end, interspersed with guilt at being relieved. Others experienced overwhelming grief and mourned the loss of their relationship, especially if caring came to an end through the death of the care recipient. Feelings of guilt were often experienced when caregiving had ended due to the care recipient's admission to a long-term care facility.

For some carers, the end of caregiving left a huge void in their life, especially if they had been providing a substantial amount of care over a number of years. Many carers were not quite sure what to do in this stage, as it took time to adjust to their changed circumstances. The 'new horizons' stage, therefore, represents new opportunities and challenges for carers as they came to terms not only with the loss of a loved one but also the loss of their role. Interactions with service providers also tended to stop at this stage. There are very few formal services other than counselling and bereavement support that are aimed particularly at ex-carers. Those that exist tend to be provided by the voluntary sector.

Changes over time

When contact was first made with them, all carers in the present study were in the 'going it alone' stage, which overlaps with 'gaining expertise' and 'sinking and swimming'. Of the 17 carers who took part in the entire study, some progressed through each stage of the model while others remained in the 'sinking or swimming' stage. When the study was concluded more than two years later, the majority of carers were receiving some kind of help to continue caring. Two carers, Mrs Veitch and Mrs Murphy, bypassed 'accessing services', 'carers as clients' and 'continuation of caring' by moving directly from 'sinking or swimming' to 'new horizons', having remained hidden from service providers till the end of their role. In Mrs Murphy's case the end of caregiving was due to the death of her husband. For Mrs Veitch, it was because her sister took over the caregiving role. Of the remaining carers, five were still in the 'going it alone' stage, determined that they did not need or want support from statutory providers. They continued to perceive service providers as authoritarian and intrusive, and wanted to maintain their sense of privacy and control of the situation. However, the experiences of other carers allow us to speculate that, if visited again at a later date, some of these people might no longer be hidden caregivers.

Conclusions

This book set out to increase our knowledge and understanding of why, when caregiving is portrayed as being stressful, carers continue without support from formal services. In doing so it has presented a temporal model of caregiving which illustrates the evolutionary process of caring. It has shown how caregiving can be likened to a career, with a beginning, a temporal dimension and an end, and how caregiving changes over time. It has provided insights into carers' experiences and their interactions with service providers. According to the model, most carers provide care on their own with support from service providers for at least some of their caring career. This stage of 'going it alone' can last an indeterminate length of time varying from a matter of weeks or months to many years. Hidden caring is, therefore, only one of a number of stages that carers go through, and there are specific stages in their career when carers are more receptive to service intervention.

Hidden carers continued to provide care without support because they perceived service providers as authoritarian and intrusive: they wanted to maintain control of the caregiving situation and their lives and would continue caring without support for as long as they felt able to. Gaining and maintaining control of the caregiving situation was particularly important to carers. Issues of choice and control were highlighted first by the processes by which individuals became carers. These processes revealed how the majority of respondents drifted into caring via the default pathway and felt that they had no choice and, as a result, no control over whether or not to become a carer.

Carers' desire to maintain their independence and control over their own lives was apparent both in their relationship with the person they were looking after and in their attitude towards service providers. They were aware of the power of service providers and alluded to it indirectly when talking about how service intervention might lead to a potential loss of independence and control. However, having finally accepted the offers of support, carers tried to re-establish control of their lives by either limiting the type of help they would accept, or by making their own arrangements for services. Within this relationship power and control were related to ownership of knowledge (about what services were available) and resources in the form of service interventions. By exercising their professional and legal powers, service providers determined carers' access to support. Carers did not want to be beholden to them.

The findings reported here are similar to those of others that suggest non-use of services is a more complex issue than simply a lack of information or knowledge (Grant et al., 1994; O'Connor 1995). O'Connor's (1995) study, for example, explored the meanings of service use among spouse carers who were in contact with service providers but continued to refuse offers of support. Their reasons were related to notions of independence, distrust of strangers and duty. Carers' determination to be independent and to overcome obstacles was associated with fear of losing control of their environment and perceived inadequacy. Acceptance of services implied a failure to cope, and provoked a sense of incompetence and a loss of personal control. Some of these themes have been demonstrated by other studies of carers and older people (Stalley, 1991; Parker, 1993). Stalley, for example, explored people's reasons for refusing home help services. Non-users seem to have a much greater need for control and a desire for independence. The need for control included the need to define the date and the time of the service and to determine what types of tasks would be undertaken.

Although recent legislation seeks to empower carers and is a positive step towards acknowledging the contribution they make to the care of older people, there are areas it does not address. This book has shown that the widely held assumption within the literature that non-use is due to a lack of knowledge and awareness of available services is an inadequate explanation. In addition, the link between carers' stress and the wish to use alternative sources of care is not straightforward. This study has conceptualised caregiving as a series of nine stages. It suggests that carers are more likely to accept service interventions at particular stages of caregiving. Thus, in order to meet the needs of carers more effectively, service providers should tailor interventions to specific stages in the caregiving trajectory. These stage-specific interventions should aim to enhance the skills, competence and expertise of family carers, thereby empowering them and facilitating the continuance of caregiving.

The book has also shown how difficult it is for carers to negotiate with service providers. It has shown how self-referral was the least effective way to access services. Some carers who eventually succeeded in obtaining help experienced the process as a lengthy, frustrating battle. Those who tried and failed to get help were left feeling bitter and disillusioned. However, the need for independence and control is vital to non-users' sense of well-being, and to force services upon these individuals might have unintended repercussions such as causing unnecessary distress. As we have seen, simply providing services does not ensure their acceptance. Clearly, there is scope for furthering our understanding of carers' reasons for not using formal services as a source of support.

The experiences of hidden carers do not augur well for the future of carers as key partners in providing care. These findings suggest that in order to improve support for all carers, policy needs to address more directly the complex issues surrounding caregiver interactions with service providers and their non-use or low take-up of services. It needs to consider the most effective way to remove barriers and facilitate access to services. Partnerships should be based on mutual respect, shared decision-making and the recognition that carers are experts. Carers and service providers will need to work together to share responsibility and to achieve mutual goals. Changing policy and practice in relation to carers will require a change in the traditional culture of service delivery, which might be challenging for providers. Legislation alone may not be enough to change the mindset and attitudes of service providers. That will take time, training, and resources.

References

Abrams, M. (1978) *Beyond Three Score and Ten,* London: Age Concern

Age Concern Institute of Gerontology (1995) *The Hidden Carers: Developing a Methodology for Deriving Local Area Profiles of Informal Carers,* London: Princess Royal Trust for Carers.

Allen, D. (2000) 'Negotiating the role of expert carers on an adult hospital ward', *Sociology of Health and Illness,* Vol. 22, No. 2, pp. 149–71

Allen, I., Hogg, D. and Peace, S. (1992) *Elderly People: Choice, Participation and Satisfaction,* London: Policy Studies Institute.

Aneshensel, C. S., Pearly, L. I., Mullan, J. T., Zarit, S. U. and Whitlach, C. J. (1995) *Profiles in Caergiving: The Unexpected Career,* San Diego, CA: Academic Press

Arber, S. and Ginn, J. (1990) 'The meaning of informal care: gender and the contribution of elderly people', *Ageing and Society,* Vol. 10, No. 4, pp. 429–54

Aronson, J. (1990) 'Women's perspectives on informal care of the elderly: ideology and personal experience of giving and receiving care', *Ageing and Society,* Vol. 10, No. 1, pp. 61–84

Ashworth, M. and Baker, A. (2000) 'Time and space: carers views about respite care', *Health and Social Care in the Community,* Vol. 8, No. 1, pp.50–6

Ashworth, M., Nafisa, M. and Corkery, M. (1996) 'Respite care in an intermediate care centre: the views of patients and carers', *Health and Social Care in the Community,* Vol. 4, No. 4, pp. 234–45

Askham, J. (1998) 'Supporting caregivers of older people: an overview of problems and priorities', *Australian Journal of Ageing,* Vol. 17, No. 1, pp. 5–7

Atkin, K. (1992) 'Similarities and differences between informal carers', in Twigg, J. (ed) (1992) *Carers Research and Practice,* London, HMSO

Banks, P. (1999) *Carer Support: Time for a Change of Direction,* London: Kings Fund

Barker, J. and Mitteness, L. (1990) 'Invisible caregivers in the spotlight: non-kin caregivers of frail older adults', in Gubrium, J. and Sankar, A. (eds) (1990) *The Home Care Experience,* London: Sage

Barnes, M. (2006) *Caring and Social Justice,* Basingstoke: Palgrave Macmillan

Bauld, L., Chesterman, J., Davies, B., Judge, K. and Mangalore, R. (2000a) *Caring for Older People: An Assessment of Community Care in the 1990s,* Aldershot: Ashgate

Bauld, L., Chesterman, J. and Judge, K. (2000b) 'Measuring satisfaction with social care amongst older service users: issues from the literature', *Health and Social Care in the Community,* Vol. 8, No. 5, pp. 316–24

Bell, D. and Bowes, A. (2006) *Financial Care Models in Scotland and the UK,* York: Joseph Rowntree Foundation

Blakemore, K. and Bonham, M. (1993) *Age, Race and Ethnicity: A Comparative Approach,* Buckingham: Open University Press

Boneham, M., Williams, K., Copeland, J., McKibbin, P., Wilson, K., Scott, A. and Saunders, P. (1997) 'Elderly people from ethnic minorities in Liverpool: mental illness, unmet need and barriers to service use', *Health and Social Care in the Community,* Vol. 5, No. 3, pp. 162–72

Boniface, D. and Denham, M. (1997) 'Factors influencing the use of community health and social services by those aged 65 and over', *Health and Social Care in the Community,* Vol. 5, No. 1, pp. 48–54

Boss, P. (1993) 'Boundary ambiguity: a block to cognitive coping', in Turnbull, A., Patterson, J., Behr, S., Murphy, D., Marquis, J. and Blue-Banning, M. (eds) *Cognitive Coping, Families and Disability*, Baltimore: Paul Brookes

Braithwaite, V. (2000) 'Contextual or genetic stress outcomes: making choices through caregiving appraisals', *The Gerontologist*, Vol. 40, No. 6, pp. 706–17

Brereton, L. and Nolan, M. (2000) 'You do know he's had a stroke don't you? Preparation for family caregiving, the neglected dimension', *Journal of Clinical Nursing*, Vol. 9, No. 4, pp. 498–506

Burholt, V., Wenger, G. C. and Scott, A. (1997) 'Dementia, disability and contact with formal services: a comparison of dementia sufferers and non-sufferers in rural and urban settings', *Health and Social Care in the Community*, Vol. 5, No. 6, pp. 384–97

Bytheway, B. and Johnson, J. (1998) 'The social construction of carers', in Symonds, A. and Kelly, A. (eds) (1998) *The Social Construction of Community Care*, Basingstoke: Macmillan

Carers Scotland (2006) *Ten Facts About Caring*, Glasgow: Carers Scotland. Available from URL: www.carerscotland.org/Aboutus/Tenfactsaboutcaring (accessed 20 August 2006)

Caserta, M., Lund, D., Wright, S. and Redbum, D. (1987) 'Caregivers to dementia patients: the utilisation of community services', *The Gerontologist*, Vol. 27, No. 2, pp. 209–14

Chapman, P. (1997) *Unmet Needs and the Delivery of Care*, Occasional Papers on Social Administration No. 61, Birkenhead: Social Administration Research Trust

Chappell, N. (1990) 'Ageing and social care', in Bibstock, R. and George, L. (eds) *Ageing and the Social Sciences*, New York: Academic Press

Charlesworth, A., Wilkin, D. and Durie, A. (1983) *Carers and Services: A Comparison of Men and Women Caring for Dependent Elderly People*, University of Manchester, Departments of Psychiatry and Community Medicine

Clarke, C. (1999) 'Partnerships in dementia care: taking it forward', in Adams, T. and Clarke, C. (eds) (1999) *Dementia Care: Developing Partnerships in Practice*, London: Bailliere Tindall

Clarke, C., Chaston, D. and Grant, G. (2003) 'Early interventions in dementia: carer-led evaluations', in Nolan, M., Lundh, L., Grant, G. and Keady, J. (eds) *Partnerships in Family Care: Understanding the Caregiving Career*, Maidenhead: Open University Press

Clarkson, P. and McCrone, P. (1998) 'Quality of life and service utilisation in South London: the PRISM of psychotic patients study', *Journal of Mental Health*, Vol. 7, No. 1, pp. 71–80

Cox, E. and Dooley, A. (1996) 'Care receivers' perceptions of their role in the care process', *Journal of Gerontological Social Work*, Vol. 26, No. 1/2, pp. 133–52

Crossroads (2001) 'A survey of carers by carers', Crossroads (Dalriada and the Isles) and Argyll and Bute Council

Curtice, L., Petch, A., Hallam, A. and Knapp, M. (2002) *Over the Threshold? An Exploration of Intensive Domiciliary Support for Older People*, Edinburgh: Scottish Executive Central Research Unit

Davidson, N. and Reed, J. (1995) 'One foot on the escalator: elderly people in sheltered accommodation', in Heywood, B. (ed) *Researching User Perspectives on Community Health Care*, London: Chapman and Hall

Department of Health (1989) *Caring for People*, London: Stationery Office

Department of Health (1999) *Caring about Carers: National Strategy for Carers*, London: Stationery Office

DHSS (Department of Health and Social Security) (1981) *Growing Older*, London, HMSO

Eagles, J., Craig, A., Rawlinson, F., Restall, D., Beattie, J. and Besson, J. (1987) 'The psychological well-being of supporters of the demented elderly', *British Journal of Psychiatry*, Vol. 150, No. 3, pp. 293–8

Eley, S. (2003) 'Diversity among carers', in Stalker, K. (ed.) *Reconceptualising Work with Carers: New Directions for Policy and Practice*, Research Highlights in Social Work No. 43, London: Jessica Kingsley

Equal Opportunities Commission (1980) *The Experience of Caring for Elderly Handicapped Dependants*, Manchester: Equal Opportunities Commission

Eraut, M. (1994) *Developing Professional Knowledge and Competence*, London: Falmer Press

Evandrou, M. (1990) *Challenging the Invisibility of Carers: Mapping Informal Care Nationally*, London: London School of Economics

Evandrou, M. (1995) 'Employment and care, paid and unpaid work: the socio-economic position of informal carers in Britain', in Phillips, J. (ed.) *Working Carers*, Avebury: Aldershot

Evandrou, M. (1996) 'Unpaid work, carers and health', in Blane, D., Brunner, E. and Wilkinson, R. (eds) (1996) *Health and Social Organisation: Towards a Health Policy for the Twenty-first Century*, London: Routledge

Finch, J. and Groves, D. (1983) *A Labour of Love: Women, Work and Caring*, London: Routledge and Kegan Paul

Foster, P. (1983) *Access to Welfare*, London: Macmillan Press

Foucault, M. (1979) *The History of Sexuality, Volume 1, An Introduction*, London: Allen Lane

George, L. (1986) 'Caregiver burden: conflict between norms of reciprocity and solidarity', in Pillemer, K. and Wolf, R. (eds) (1986) *Elder Abuse: Conflict in the Family*, Massachusetts: Auburn

George, L. and Gwyther, L. (1986) 'Caregiver well-being: a multidimensional examination of family caregivers of demented adults', *The Gerontologist*, Vol. 26, No. 3, pp. 253–9

Geraedts, M., Heller, G. and Harrington, C. (2000) 'Germany's long term care insurance: putting a social insurance model into practice', *The Milbank Quarterly*, Vol. 78, No. 3, pp. 375–401

Gilhooly, M. (1987) 'Senile dementia and the family', in Orford, J. (ed) (1987) *Coping with Disorder in the Family*, London: Croom Helm

Gilleard, C. J. (1987) 'Influence of emotional distress amongst supporters on the outcomes of psychogeriatric day care', *British Journal of Psychiatry*, Vol. 150, No. 2, pp. 214–23

Gillies, B. (2000) 'Acting up: role ambiguity and the legal recognition of carers', *Ageing and Society*, Vol. 20, No. 4, pp 429–44

Gouldner, A. (1973) 'The norm of reciprocity', *American Sociological Review*, Vol. 25, No. 2, pp 161–78

Graham, H. (1983) 'Caring: a labour of love', in Finch, J. and Groves, D. (eds) (1983) *A Labour of Love: Women, Work and Caring*, London: Routlegde and Kegan Paul

Grant, G. (2001) 'Older people with learning difficulties: health, community inclusion and family caregiving', in Nolan, M., Davies, S. and Grant, G. (eds) (2001) *Working with Older People and their Families: Key Issues in Policy and Practice*, Buckingham: Open University Press

Grant, G., McGrath, M. and Ramcharan, P. (1994) 'How family and informal supporters appraise service quality', *International Journal of Disability, Development and Education*, Vol. 41, No. 2, pp. 127–41

Green, H. (1988) *Informal Carers: General Household Survey 1985*, OPCS. London: HMSO

Gunaratnam, Y. (1997) 'Breaking the silence: black and ethnic minority carers and service provision', in Bornat, J., Johnson, J., Pereira, C., Pilgrim, D. and Williams, F. (eds) (1997) *Community Care: A Reader*, London: Macmillan/Open University

Hardy, B., Young, R. and Wistow, G. (1999) 'Dimensions of choice in the assessment and care management process: the views of older people, carers and care managers', *Health and Social Care in the Community*, Vol. 7, No. 6, pp. 475–82

Heyman, B. (1995) *Researching User Perspectives on Community Health Care*, London: Chapman and Hall

Hogg, C. (1999) *Patients, Power and Politics: From Patients to Citizens*, London: Sage

Howard, M. (2001) *Paying the Price: Carers, Poverty and Social Exclusion*, London: Child Poverty Action Group/Carers UK

Hugman, R. (1991) *Power in Caring Professions*, Basingstoke: Macmillan

Hutton, S. and Hirst, M. (2001) *Caring Relationships Over Time*, University of York: Social Policy Research Unit

Jarrett, N., Payne, S. and Wiles, R. (1999) 'Terminally ill patients' and lay carers' perceptions and experiences of community based services, *Journal of Advanced Nursing*, Vol. 29, No. 2, pp. 467–83

Jutras, S. and Veilleux, F. (1991) 'Informal caregiving: correlates of perceived burden', *Canadian Journal on Ageing*, Vol. 10, No. 1, pp. 40–55

Kahana, E. and Young, R. (1990) 'Clarifying the caregiver paradigm: challenges for the future', in Beigel, D, and Blum, A. (eds) (1990) *Ageing and Caregiving Theory: Research and Policy*, Newbury Park, CA: Sage

Keady, J. and Nolan, M. (1993) 'The carer-led assessment process (CLASP): a framework for the assessment of need in dementia caregivers', *Journal of Clinical Nursing*, Vol. 3, No. 2, pp 103–8

Keady, J. and Nolan, M. R. (1995) 'IMMEL: assessing coping responses in the early stages of dementia', *British Journal of Nursing*, Vol. 4, No. 7, pp. 377–80

Langan, J., Whitfield, M. and Russell, O. (1995) 'Paid and unpaid carers: their role in and satisfaction with primary health care for people with learning disabilities', *Health and Social Care*, Vol. 2, No. 6, pp. 357–65

Lazarus, R. (1991) 'Coping theory and research: past, recent and future', *Psychosomatic Medicine*, Vol. 55: No. 3, pp. 234–47

Lazarus, R. S. and Folkman, S. (1984) *Stress, Appraisal and Coping,* New York: Springer

Leininger, M. (1981) *Caring: An Essential Human Need*, New Jersey: Charles Slack

Levin, E., Moriarty, J. and Gorbach, P. (1994) *Better for the Break*, London: HMSO

Lewis, J. and Meredith, B. (1988) *Daughters Who Care*, London: Routledge

Llewellyn, G. (2003) 'Family care decision-making in later life: the future is now!', in Nolan, M., Lundh, L., Grant, G. and Keady, J. (eds) *Partnerships in Family Care: Understanding the Caregiving Career*, Maidenhead: Open University Press

Lloyd, L. (2000) 'Caring about carers: only half the picture?' *Critical Social Policy*, Vol. 20, No. 1, pp. 136–50

Lukes, S. (1987) *Power*, Oxford: Blackwell

McDonald, C. (1999) *Support at Home: Views of Older People about their Needs and Access to Services*, Edinburgh: Scottish Executive Central Research Unit

McDonald, C. (2004) *Older People and Community Care in Scotland: A Review of Recent Research*, Edinburgh: Scottish Executive Social Research

Maher, J. and Green, H. (2002) *Carers 2000: Results from the Carers Module of the National Household Survey 2000*, London: Stationery Office

Montgomery, R. and Kosloski, K. (2000) 'Family caregiving: change, continuity and diversity', in Lawton, M. P. and Rubestein, R. (eds) *Interventions in Dementia Care: Towards Improving Quality of Life*, New York: Springer

Motenko, A. (1989) 'The frustrations, gratifications and well-being of dementia caregivers', *The Gerontologist*, Vol. 29, No. 2, pp 166–72

Mudge, K. and Ratcliffe, I. (1995) 'Considering the needs of carers: a survey of their views on services', *Journal of Advanced Nursing*, Vol. 9, No. 1, pp. 29–31

Murphy, B., Schofield, H., Bloch, S., Herrman, H. and Singh, B. (1997) 'Women with multiple roles: the emotional impact of caring for ageing parents', *Ageing and Society*, Vol. 17, No. 3, pp. 277–91

Murray, J. and Livingston, G. (1998) 'A qualitative study of adjustment to caring for an older spouse with psychiatric illness', *Ageing and Society*, Vol. 18, No. 6, pp. 659–71

Myers, F. and McDonald, C. (1996) 'Power to the people? Involving users and carers in needs assessments and care planning: views from the practitioner', *Health and Social Care in the Community*, Vol. 4, No. 1, pp. 86–95

Nissel, M. and Bonnerjea, A. (1982) *Family Care of the Handicapped Elderly: Who Pays?* London: Policy Studies Institute

Nocon, A. and Qureshi, H. (1996) *Outcomes of Community Care for Users and Carers: A Social Service Perspective*, Buckingham: Open University Press

Noddings, N. (1984) *Caring: A Feminist Approach to Ethics and Moral Education*, Berkeley, CA: University of California Press

Nolan, M. (1993) 'Carer/dependant relationships and the prevention of elder abuse', in Delcalmer, P. and Glendinning, F. (eds) (1993) *The Abuse and Neglect of Elderly People: A Handbook*, London: Sage Publications.

Nolan, M. and Grant, G. (1992)*Regular Respite: An Evaluation of a Hospital Rota Bed System for Elderly People*, Age Concern Institute of Gerontology Research Papers, Series No. 6, London: Ace Books

Nolan, M., Davies, S. and Grant, G. (2001) *Working with Older People and Their Families: Key Issues in Policy and Practice,* Buckingham: Open University Press

Nolan, M., Grant, G. and Keady, J. (1996) *Understanding Family Care: A Multidimensional Model of Caring and Coping*, Buckingham: Open University Press

Nolan, M., Lundh, L., Grant, G. and Keady, J. (2003) *Partnerships in Family Care: Understanding the Caregiving Career*, Maidenhead: Open University Press

O'Connor, D. (1995) 'Supporting spousal caregivers: exploring the meaning of service use', *Journal of Contemporary Human Services*, Vol. 76, No. 3, pp. 296-305

Opie, A. (1994) 'The instability of the caring body: gender and caregivers of older people', *Qualitative Health Research*, Vol. 4, No. 1, pp. 31–50

Orme, J. (2001) *Gender and Community Care*, Basingstoke: Palgrave

Pahl, J. (1989) *Money and Marriage*, Basingstoke: Macmillan

Parker, G. (1990) *With Due Care and Attention: A Review of Research on Informal Care*, London: Family Policy Studies Centre

Parker, G. (1993) *With This Body: Caring and Disability in Marriage*, Buckingham, Open University Press

Parker, G. and Clarke, H. (2002) 'Making the ends meet: do carers and disabled people have a common agenda?', *Policy and Politics*, Vol. 30, No. 3, pp. 347–59

Pearlin, L. (1991) 'The study of coping: an overview of problems and directions', in Eckenrode, J. (ed.) (1991) *The Social Context of Coping*, New York: Plenum Press.

Pearlin, L., Harrington, C., Powell-Lawton, M. and Zarit, S. (2001) 'An overview of the social and behavioural consequences of Alzheimer's disease', *Aging and Mental Health*, Vol. 5, Supplement 1, pp. S3–S6

Pearlin, L., Mullan, J., Semple, S. and Skaff, M. (1990) 'Caregiving and the stress process: an overview of concepts and their measures', *The Gerontologist*, Vol. 30, No. 5, pp. 583-94

Perring, C., Twigg, J. and Atkin, K. (1990) *Families Caring for People Diagnosed as Mentally Ill: The Literature Re-examined*, London: HMSO

Phillips, P. (1993) 'A deconstruction of caring', *Journal of Advanced Nursing*, Vol. 18, No. 10, pp. 1554–58

Pitkeathley, J. (1989) *It's My Duty, Isn't It? The Plight of Carers in Our Society,* London: Souvenir Press

Pitkeathley, J. (1994) 'Safeguarding the carers', in Davidson, R. and Hunter, S. (eds) (1994) *Community Care in Practice*, London: Batsford

Princess Royal Trust for Carers (1998a) *Eight Hours a Day and Taken for Granted*, London: PRTC

Princess Royal Trust for Carers (1998b) *How Do Communities Care?* Inverness: PRTC

Princess Royal Trust for Carers (1999) *'Seven and half minutes is not enough' Working together to support carers — a good practice guide for carers support workers and GP practices*, London, PRTC.

Qureshi, H. and Walker, A. (1989) *The Caring Relationship*, Basingstoke: Macmillan Educational

Raynes, N., Temple, B., Glenister, C. and Coulthard, L. (2001) *Quality at Home for Older People: Involving Service Users in Defining Home Care Specifications*, Bristol: Policy Press

Royal Commission on Long Term Care (1999) *With Respect to Old Age: Long Term Care –*

Rights and Responsibilities, London: Stationery Office

Schofield, H., Murphy, B., Herrman, H., Bloch, S. and Singh, B. (1998) 'Carers of people aged over 50 with physical impairment, memory loss and dementia: a comparative study', *Ageing and Society*, Vol. 18, No. 3, pp. 355–69

Scottish Executive (1999) *National Strategy for Carers*, Edinburgh: Stationery Office

Scottish Executive (2001a) *Fair Care for Older People: Report of the Care Development Group*, Edinburgh: Stationery Office

Scottish Executive (2001b) *Report of the Scottish Carers Legislation Working Group*, Edinburgh: Stationery Office

Scottish Executive (2005) *Delivering for Health*, Edinburgh: Scottish Executive

Scottish Executive (2006a) *The Future of Unpaid Care in Scotland*, Edinburgh: Scottish Executive

Scottish Executive (2006b) *Response to Care 21 Report: The Future of Unpaid Care in Scotland*, Edinburgh: Scottish Executive

Scottish Executive (2006c) *Changing Lives: Report of the 21st Century Review of Social Work*, Edinburgh: Scottish Executive

Simpson, R., Scotherm, G. and Mark, V. (1995) 'Survey of carers' satisfaction with the quality of care delivered to in-patients suffering from dementia', *Journal of Advanced Nursing*, Vol. 22, No. 2, pp. 517–27

Sinclair, I. (1990) 'Carers: their contribution and quality of life', in Sinclair, I., Parker, R., Leat, D. and Williams, J. (eds) (1990) *The Kaleidscope of Care: A Review of Research on Welfare Provision for Elderly People*, London: HMSO

Sinclair, I. (1994) 'On the receiving end: elderly consumers' perceptions of community care', in Davidson, R. and Hunter, S. (eds) (1994) *Community Care in Practice*, London: Batsford

Stalker, K., Cadogan, L., Petrie, M., Jones, C. and Murray, J. (1999) '*If You Don't Ask You Don't Get': A Review of Services for People with Learning Difficulties: The Views of People who Use Services and Their Carers*, Edinburgh: Scottish Office Central Research Unit

Stalley, E. (1991) 'The reluctant client: a study of elderly people who decline the home help service', unpublished MSc thesis, University of Glasgow

Statham, J. (2003) 'A day at a time: a study of unsupported family carers of older people', unpublished PhD thesis, University of Glasgow

Stearns, S. and Butterworth, S. (2001) *Demand for and Utilisation of Personal Care Services for the Elderly*, Health and Community Care Research Findings No. 7, Edinburgh: Scottish Executive Central Research Unit

Tamborrelli, P. (1993) 'Exemplar A: becoming a carer', in Gilbert, N. (ed.) (1993) *Researching Social Life*, London: Sage

Taylor, R. and Ford, G. (1994) *Caring in the Community: A Study of Carers in the East End of Glasgow*, Glasgow: The Princess Royal Trust Glasgow East End Community Carers Centre

Thompson, E., Futterman, A., Thompson, D., Rose, J. and Lovett, S. (1993) 'Social support and caregiving burden in family caregivers of frail elders', *Journal of Gerontology*, Vol. 48, No. 5, pp. 245–54

Tinker, A. (1997) *Older People in Modern Society*, London: Longman

Twigg, J. (1989) 'Models of carers: how do social care agencies conceptualise their relationship with informal carers?', *Journal of Social Policy*, Vol. 18, No. 1, pp. 53–66

Twigg, J. (1992) *Carers: Research and Practice*, London: HMSO

Twigg, J. (2000) *Bathing: The Body and Community Care*, London: Routledge

Twigg, J. and Atkin, K. (1993) 'Integrating carers into the service system: six strategic responses', *Ageing and Society*, Vol. 13, No. 2, pp. 141–70

Twigg, J. and Atkin, K. (1994) *Carers Perceived: Policy and Practice in Informal Care*, Buckingham: Open University Press

Twigg, J., Atkin, K., Perring, C. (1990) *Carers and Services: A Review of Research*, London: HMSO

Ungerson, C. (1983) 'Women and caring: skills, tasks and taboos', in Garmanikow, E.,

Morgan, D., Purvis, J. and Taylorson, D. (eds) (1983) *The Public and the Private*, London: Heineman

Ungerson, C. (1987) *Policy is Personal*, London: Tavistock

Warner, N. (1995) *Better Tomorrows*, London: Carers National Association

Webb, C. (1996) 'Caring, curing and coping', in Heller, T., Muston, R., Sidell, M. and Lloyd, C. (eds) (2001) *Working for Health*, London: Open University/Sage

Wenger, C. G. (1990) 'Elderly carers: the need for appropriate intervention', *Ageing and Society*, Vol. 10, No. 2, pp. 197–219

Willoughby, J. and Keating, N. (1991) 'Being in control: the process of caring for a relative with Alzheimer's Disease', *Qualitative Health Research*, Vol. 1, No. 1, pp. 27–50

Wilson, E. (1977) *Women and the Welfare State*, London: Tavistock

Wilson, G. (1995) *Community Care: Asking the Users*, London, Chapman Hall

Wilson, H. S. (1989) 'Family caregiving for a relative with Alzheimer's dementia: coping with negative choices', *Nursing Research*, Vol. 38, No. 2, pp. 94–8

Wright, F. (1986) *Left to Care Alone*, Aldershot: Gower

Wright, F. (2000) 'Continuing to pay: the consequences for family caregivers of an older person's admission to a care home', *Social Policy and Administration*, Vol. 34, No. 2, pp. 191–205

Wuest, J. (2000) 'Repatterning care: women's proactive management of family caregiving demands', *Health Care for Women International*, Vol. 21, No. 5, pp. 393–411

Internet resources

Carers and Disabled Children Act 2000. Available from URL: www.hmso.gov.uk/acts/acts2000/20000016.htm (accessed 9 August 2006)

Community Care and Health (Scotland) Act 2002. Available from URL: www.scotland.gov.uk/Topics/Health/care/17655/9803 (20 Aug 2006)

Carers (Equal Opportunities) Act (2004). Available from URL: www.carersuk.org./Policyand-practice/CarersEqualOpportunitiesAct (accessed 25 April 2006)

Federal Ministry of Health and Social Security, Germany. URL: www.bmgs.bund.de (accessed 9 August 2006)

Ministry for Social Affairs, Denmark. URL: http://eng.social.dk/ministry.html (accessed 20 August 2006)

Ministry of the Interior and Health, Denmark. URL: http://www.im.dk/Index/mainstart.asp?o=2&n=3&s=5 (accessed 9 August 2006)

Scotland's Census Results Online (SCROL). Available from URL: www.scrol.gov.uk (accessed 9 August 2006)

Scottish Community Care Statistics. Available from URL: www.scotland.gov.uk/topics/statistics/ (accessed 20 August 2006)

Index

Abrams, M. 2
accommodation factors 38–9
affection 24, 25, 26
Allen, D. 61
Arber, S. 1
assertiveness 59
assessment: cross-agency 10; process 60;
    right to 5, 7, 8, 11–12, 55, 70–1; *see*
    also referral and assessment procedure
Atkin, K. 29, 40–1, 46–7
autonomy 30–1

behavioural responses 37–8
boundary-setting 46
Bytheway, B. 1, 4

care assistants 2
care attendants 2
Care Commission 10
cared-for: and carers ix, 30–5,
    64–5; discharge from hospital 55;
    improvements in condition 40; non-use
    of support services 17–19, 49–52, 74
caregiving 19–22; caring activities 27–9;
    continuation 70–1; control of 30–5;
    costs 1, 4; free 8–9; house rules 30–5;
    long-term 4, 34; policymakers 1;
    positive outcomes 39–42, 48; stages
    of 21, 62–8, 74; temporal model 20–1,
    42–6, 62–73
carer support groups 17, 56
carers ix; assessment entitlement 5, 7, 8,
    11–12, 55, 70–1; assuming role 23–5,
    63–4; autonomy 30–1; balanced 46;
    and cared-for ix, 30–5, 64–5; changes
    over time 72; as clients 22, 49, 61,
    69–70; control 61, 67; coping strategies
    ix, 36–8, 66–8; devolution impact 5–11;
    employment leave 13; engulfed 46–7;
    gaining expertise 43–4, 46–8, 65–6;
    health/training 2, 10; identifying 1–4;
    informal 2, 3, 4; local authorities 7, 11;
    non-resident 31; response to crisis 46–
    8; self-reliance 19; service providers
    15, 16–17, 18–19, 22, 60–1; social
    identity 4; statistics ix, 23; support for

4, 9, 13–14, 16–17, 51, 68; symbiotic
    47; terminally ill people 13; *see also*
    family carers; hidden carers; young
    carers
Carers Allowance 32
Carers and Disabled Children Act (2000)
    11–12
Carers (Equal Opportunities) Act (2004)
    11
Carers National Association 2
Carers Scotland 66
Carers (Services and Recognition) Act
    (1995) 5, 6, 7–8, 11
Carers Strategy 6, 64
Caring about Carers (DoH) 6
Caring for People White Paper 3, 4
case closure system 59
Changing Lives (Scottish Executive) 65,
    68
Chappell, N. 24
choice 23–5, 27, 63–4
community care 1, 2–3
Community Care and Health (Scotland)
    Act (2002) 8–9, 64, 69, 71
community nursing staff 50–1
conflict situations 29, 32–3, 41–2, 61
Conservatives 2–3
control: of caregiving 30–5; carers 50–1,
    61, 67; hidden carers 73; non-users 74
coping: accommodation factors 38–9;
    crises 67; outcomes 39–42, 48;
    resources 38–9; strategies ix, 36–8,
    66–8; temporal factors 42–6
co-residency 24–5, 34
costs of care 1, 4
crises: appraisal 45; carers' response
    46–8; coping 67; hidden carers 44–6;
    transition to support 56–7
cross-agency assessment 10
Curtice, L. 17

daughters as carers 24, 26, 27, 28–9
Davidson, N. 59
day care, access to 58
decision-making 32–3, 61, 63
delays in service provision 53, 59

Delivering for Health (Scottish Executive) 11
demanding behaviour 67
dementia sufferers 20, 67
Denmark 12–13, 14
Department of Health: *Caring about Carers* 6
Department of Health and Social Security 3
dependency 59, 61
depression 41–2
devolution impact on carers 5–11
duty 24, 27

employment leave 13
England, legislation on carers 11–12
Equal Opportunities Commission 2
equipment 38–9, 57
Eraut, M. 43–4
ethnic minorities 17
expertise, development of 43–4, 46–8, 65–6

family carers 21–2; *see also* daughters as carers; sibling carers; sons as carers; spouse carers
feminist critiques of community care 3
financial factors 31–2
Ford, G. 17
Foucault, M. 60
free personal and nursing care 8–9
The Future of Unpaid Care in Scotland (Scottish Executive) 9–11, 66

gender factors, intimate care 28–9
General Household Survey 17
general practitioners 53–5, 57
Germany 12, 13–14
Gilhooley, M. 67
Ginn, J. 1
Gouldner, A. 26
Grant, G. 19, 20
Growing Older White Paper 2–3
guilt 33–4, 72

health, social care 4–5
health records, access 10
Her Majesty's Inspectorate of Education 10
hidden carers vi, ix–x; caring activities 27–9; control 73; crises 44–6; general practitioners 53–5; identifying 15–16; overload 44–5; own family problems 41–2, 60; problem-solving 36–8;

reasons 73; service providers 49; as service users 52–6; stages in developing 23–5, 63–8; *see also* stress; temporal model of caregiving
home care service providers 12
home ownership 30–5, 50–1, 65
hospital discharge 55

identity 4, 60, 61
incontinence 28, 29, 36, 38–9, 67
independence 38–9, 73, 74
information, service provision 18–19
institutional care 40
intensive support packages 17
interdependence 31
intimate care 28–9
intrusion 50–1, 57, 61, 69–70
Invalid Care Allowance 3

Johnson, J. 1, 4

Keady, J. 20
Keating, N. 20

Labour 6
learning disabilities, people with 17
local authorities 7, 11
Long Term Care Insurance 12, 13–14
love 24, 25

marriage 24; *see also* spouse carers
mental health services 17
Motenko, A. 42
motivation 24, 25–7
music 38

National Association for Carers 2
National Council for Carers and their Elderly Dependants 2
National Council for the Single Woman and her Dependants 2
NHS and Community Care Act (1990) 4–5
Nolan, M. 20, 42
non-users: older people 17–19; reasons 49–52, 74; *see also* hidden carers

obligation 24, 25, 26–7
older people: free personal and nursing care 8–9; non-use of support services 17–19; professionals 18–19
outcomes: negative 40; positive 39–42, 48
overload 44–5; *see also* stress

84   Index

Pahl, J. 32
parental authority 30–2, 34
partnership approach: carers/service providers 61, 62, 74; lacking 70; legislation 71; Scotland 14
personal care 8–9, 27–9
person-centred approach 65
physical care 27–9
pleasure in caring 39–40
policymakers 1
power dynamics 60–1; see also conflict situations; control
pressure groups 2
preventative approach 67–8
privacy 51, 61, 70
problem-solving 36–8
professionals 18–19

quasi-market approach 4

reciprocity 25, 26
Reed, J. 59
referral and assessment procedure 53, 59; see also self-referral
residential homes 27
respite care 10, 11, 17, 58, 70
restrictions on life 40–2
Review of Nursing in the Community 10
routines, changing 70
Royal Commission on Long Term Care 8, 9

Scotland: carer statistics 23; carers as key partners 14; devolution impact 5–11
Scottish Carers Legislation Working Group (Scottish Executive) 7–8, 70
Scottish Executive: Changing Lives 65, 68; Delivering for Health 11; The Future of Unpaid Care in Scotland 9–11, 66; Scottish Carers Legislation Working Group 7–8, 70; Strategy for Carers in Scotland 6; support initiatives 5, 9–11
Scottish Parliament 8–9
self-appraisal 45–6
self-care 28
self-referral 52–3, 68, 74
self-reliance 19
service interventions, temporal mode 62–72
service providers: authoritarian 50, 57; and carers 15, 16–17, 18–19, 22, 60–1; criticisms of 64, 70; hidden carers 49; intrusion 50–1, 57, 61, 69–70

service provision: acceptance of 73–4; access to 68–9, 71; criticisms 58–60; delays 53, 59; experience of 57–60; history of use 19; inflexibility 18; information 18–19; tensions 70; used by carers 17–19
short-term break voucher 11
sibling carers 26, 27, 43
Simpson, R. 18
social care 4–5
social isolation 40
Social Work Inspection Agency 10
social work practice 58
sons as carers 24, 26, 27, 28–9
spouse carers 3, 24, 26, 27, 28, 47, 63, 73
Stalley, E. 74
Strategy for Carers in Scotland (Scottish Executive) 6
stress ix, 17, 36; behavioural responses 37–8; increasing 42–3, 66–7; passivity 46; perceptions of 48; temporal factors 42–6
support for carers: cared-for 51; Denmark 13, 14; Germany 13–14; legislation 4; policy for informal carers 16–17; preventative approach 68; Scottish Executive 5, 9–11; training 68
surveillance techniques 41, 61

Taylor, R. 17
temporal model of caregiving 20–1, 72–3; acceptance of role 63–4; accessing services 68–9; carers/clients 69–70; continuation 70–1; coping 42–6; dawning realisation 62–3; going it alone 64–5; new horizons 71–2; sinking/swimming 66–8; stress 42–6
tensions in service provision 70
terminally ill people 13
threats 34
training opportunities 10, 66
transition to support 56–7
Twigg, J. 16–17, 29, 40–1, 46–7

United Kingdom policy 2–3, 4–5

welfare 2–3, 4–5, 18; Denmark 12–13; Germany 13–14; Labour 6
Willoughby, J. 20
Wilson, H. S. 20
Working for Patients White Paper 4

young carers 10, 11